THE SHILOAH CENTER FOR MIDDLE EASTERN AND AFRICAN STUDIES

OCCASIONAL PAPERS SERIES

INVOLVEMENT, INVASION AND WITHDRAWAL: QADHDHĀFĪ'S LIBYA AND CHAD, 1969-1981

INVOLVEMENT, INVASION AND WITHDRAWAL: QADHDHĀFĪ'S LIBYA AND CHAD, 1969-1981

BENYAMIN NEUBERGER

Published by the Shiloah Center for Middle Eastern and African Studies
Tel-Aviv University

ISBN 965-224-002-8

CONTENTS

PREFACE

The research project which produced this paper was undertaken in November 1980. One month later, Libyan tanks rolled into Chad's capital and, on January 6, 1981, the Libya-Chad Union was proclaimed. The theme of Libyan-Chadian relations is significant, reflecting the tensions between Arab North Africa and sub-Saharan Black Africa and enabling us to study Qadhdhāfī's foreign policy. The paper analyses the historical connection between Libya and Chad, the complex link between internal Chadian politics and the Libyan involvement and Libya's policies in Chad as part of Qadhdhāfī's 'Grand Strategy' in the African and Arab World.

I wish to thank all those who made the publication of this research possible — in particular Prof. Itamar Rabinovich, Mr. Daniel Dishon and Ms. Edna Liftman of the Shiloah Center for Middle Eastern and African Studies. Thanks also to Dr. Michael Lasker who specializes in North African affairs and who discussed the research project with me. Ms. Ofra Bengio of the Shiloah Center read the manuscript, made important suggestions and helped me with the transliteration of the Arab names. I wish to thank Ms. Helen Silman for her perceptive and helpful editorial work and Ms. Ruth Beit-Or for producing the maps which make the text so much easier to understand. I would like to dedicate this paper to my mother, Ilse Neuberger, who taught me to hate war and oppression.

B.N.

I

CHAD: THE INTERNAL SETTING

The recent Libyan invasion and quasi-occupation of Chad can only be understood by analysing the complexities and intricacies of Chadian history. The ethnic and religious antagonism between the peoples of Chad, the twenty years of civil war between the North and the South, the recent struggle within the Muslim North and the Arab and the Libyan involvement have their roots in pre-colonial times and in the peculiar geographic and demographic conditions of Chad.

Chad is a huge African state of 1,284,000 sq. km, but it is thinly populated by four million people. A good part of its problems in achieving a modicum of national cohesion stems from its enormous size. Thus, the distance from Aouzou in the North to Baibakoum in the South is equivalent to a straight line from Oslo to the Mediterranean. Chad is also a landlocked country, and its nearest ports in Nigeria and Cameroun are more than 2,500 km to the south. Its neighbours are two Arab states (Libya and Sudan) and five black African nations (Niger, Mali, Nigeria, Cameroun and the Central African Republic). It sits uneasily within two civilizations — the Arab-Islamic and Black African. The bloody conflicts in recent Chadian history reflect the competing pushes and pulls of Arab North Africa and Francophone Black Africa.

The country is basically divided into two parts, the "Two Chads", which are separated by the Chari river. The North, which is sub-divided into the Sahara desert region, called B.E.T. (Borkou–Ennedi–Tibesti), and the dry Sahel region, is almost completely Muslim. The South — geographically a rainy forest savannah — is equally divided between Christians and Pagans. Chadian Islam is very much politicised and Arabised and thus very different from the non-political Islam of the other Francophone Black African states.[1] The pull between the Arabised Muslim North, which has strong historical religious and emotional links with the Arab world, and the South, which regards itself as part of Black Africa, is enormous. Only in the Sudan is there a similar

9

north-south polarisation, while in other Sahel states like Mali, Niger and Mauritiania, Islam serves as a unifying bond between the "white" Sahara region, inhabited by Arabs, Berbers and Touaregs, and the "black" Sahel region.

An important difference between North and South is in the life-style of the populations. In the North a part of the population is nomadic or semi-sedentary, while in the South all the peoples are agrarian and sedentary. The economy of the North is based on livestock raising, while the South is cultivating cotton which earns up to 80% of Chad's export income.

The dividing line between the Muslim North and the Christian-pagan South is also the boundary between "Cotton Chad" and "Cattle Chad". While the North comprises four-fifths of Chad's territory, one half of Chad's population resides in the populated south-west. In the South about half of the school-age children go to school, while in the North only about 3% acquire some kind of modern education.[2]

The ethnic map of Chad is complex, consisting of dozens of different peoples who have their own territory, history, culture and language. The reason for this extreme ethnic diversity lies in the numerous migration waves throughout history from east to west and from north to south; in the intermingling of Arab invaders with native peoples and in the widespread slave hunting in the last centuries. New "tribes" were constantly created by these dynamic historical processes.

In the Saharan North the dominant ethnic group is the Toubou nomads, who are divided into two main sub-divisions: the homogeneous Teda of Tibesti and the heterogeneous Daza (or Goranes) of Borkou and Ennedi who consist of various tribes (Anakaza, Doza, etc.). Both groups have close connections with their fellow Toubous in Niger and Libya. This division is important in understanding the split, in the late 1970s, between pro- and anti-Libyan factions among the Toubous. The most important groupings in the Sahel are the Ouaddaian tribes, the Arab tribes (Hassouna, Djohuina, Ouled Sliman), the Kanembou and the Hadjerai. The *lingua franca* in the Saharan and Sahelian North is Arabic: The African South is completely dominated by the Sara which constitute the largest ethnic group in the whole of Chad (30%).

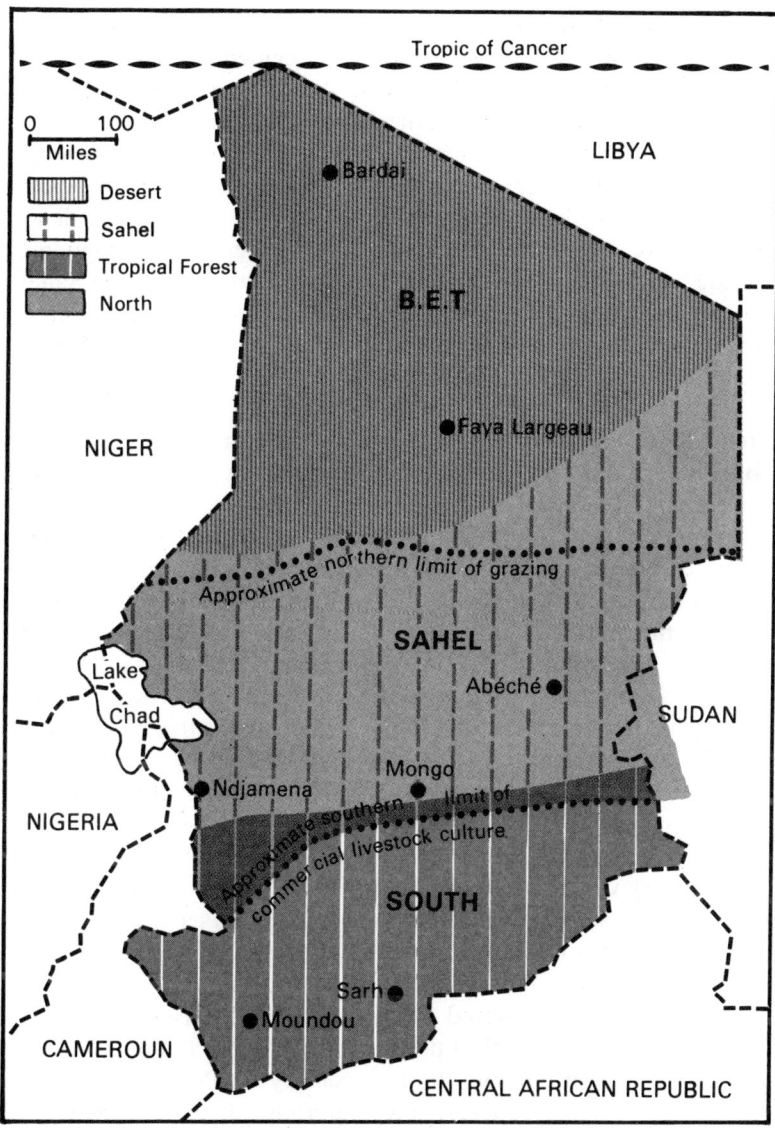

Map No 1: The Regions of Chad

The pre-colonial background of north and south Chad is completely different. The South was segmentary and without states, whereas in the Sahelian North the strong Muslim kingdoms of Kanem, Quaddai and Baguirmi dominated the whole area. In the 18th and 19th centuries, wars between the three kingdoms were fought for hegemony in the Sahel area.[3] The political organization of the Saharan North was tribal — an intermediary stage between the segmentary South and the centralized kingdoms of the Sahel. Relations between the Saharan tribes and the Sahel kingdoms were tense and hostile. Thus, historically, in addition to the basic cleavage between the Muslim North and the non-Muslim South, there was a traditional rivalry within the North between the Sahara and the Sahel regions. Within the Sahel the main historical antagonism was between Quaddai in the east and Kanem and Baguirmi in the west which were overrun by the forces of Quaddai in the 19th century.

In pre-colonial times slave raiding characterized the relations between the Arabised Muslim North and the African Pagan South. For centuries, the kingdoms of Quaddai, Kanem and Baguirmi raided the Sara country in order to capture slaves for their lucrative slave trade.[4] The political structure and the economy of the Sahel states was based on raiding and trading "slave-material" from the South.[5] Because of the segmentary structure of the South, the Africans, organised in tiny villages, clans and sub-tribes, could not resist the military might of the Sahel Sultanates. Southern slaves were employed in large numbers throughout the North — the salt mines, for example, were all operated by Southern slaves. Slaves were also used as a kind of currency in the pre-colonial North, tens of thousands being sold each year by the Sahel Sultanates to the territories now comprised in Egypt, Sudan and Libya. To the present day, in many Northern tribes the lowest social strata are composed of descendants of slaves.[6]

There is ample historical documentation about the brutal trade in human lives throughout the 19th century. In 1870, the German explorer Nachigall reported the capturing of 30,000 slaves by Sultan Ali of Quaddai. Other travellers spoke of an annual export of 5,000 slaves by the Beguirmi kingdom at the turn of the century. In a book published in 1902, the German traveller von Oppenheim described how Muslim slave hunters shot down Africans hiding for refuge in high trees.[7]

Stories about the depopulation of whole areas and the destruction of entire tribes by Muslim forces are still alive among Chad's black African population. The division of Chad into the North "*Dār al-Islām*" (House of Islam) and the South "*Dār al 'Abīd*" (House of Slaves) is crucial to the understanding of the civil war in Chad in the 1960s and 1970s.

The French, who began their conquest of Chad in the late 19th century, brought about radical changes in the traditional structure of power between the Muslim North and the Pagan South. The French were received as liberators by the African South, because they put an end to the slave raiding expeditions of the Muslims. In Kanem and Baguirmi Kingdoms the French were regarded as allies in their desperate war of survival against invading forces coming from the eastern Sahel and Sudan. In Quaddai and Toubou country the French were seen as foreign invaders and infidels and until the 1920s they met there with fierce resistance. In the 1960s, those same regions were in revolt against the independent government of Chad which was regarded as a French puppet, surviving with the help of French bayonets.

The French conquest and subjugation of the North was violent and cruel. Between 1913 and 1918 the kingdom of Quaddai, for example, lost 60% of its population most of them by starvation, which was a result of the colonial conquest. This is an important reason why Quaddai became a recruitment area for the anti-French insurgents of the 1960s and 1970s. French rule also reversed the traditional commercial routes. In pre-colonial times, the major trade routes went from south to north, from Chad to Egypt, Libya, and Sudan — and the major export items were African slaves from the South. In the French era, the slave trade was suppressed and the major commercial links were from south Chad to Europe via the ports of Nigeria and Cameroun. Chad then exported cotton grown in the South, while all its imports came from the Atlantic coast. The reversal of trade routes and the suppression of slavery led to a rapid economic decline in the Muslim North.

Not only did French rule introduce commercial and foreign currency earning crops into the fertile South, but it also concentrated there all its investments. The fact that the Southern Sara were pro-French and non-Muslim facilitated the educational activity of the missions and the adoption of Christianity. The

Muslim North opposed any missionary activity and, as a result, did not enjoy the advantages of Western education. Educated Saras from the South filled all the administrative positions reserved for the indigenous population in the whole of Chad, and thousands of Saras flocked to serve in the French army. Thus, while French colonialism broke the political and military power of the North, and weakened its economy, it provided the South with economic resources, administrative skills and military power. French rule dramatically reversed the historical relationship — the former slavers were pushed into an inferior position while their erstwhile slaves acquired the skills and capabilities for ruling Chad after independence. Naturally, once the French withdrew, the North attempted to undo the unhappy colonial episode and to revert to the pre-colonial power structure.

In the post-Second World War era of anti-colonial nationalism and decolonization, hostility between north and south Chad continued unabated. In 1946, Southern teachers and civil servants founded a nationalist anti-colonial party, the *Parti Progressiste Tchadien* (PTT), led by Gabriel Lisette and Francois Tombalbaye. The French founded at the same time the *Union Démocratique Tchadienne* (UDT), which collaborated with them. The UDT, which became later the *Action Sociale Tchadienne* (AST) represented local French interests and the Northern conservative Muslim rulers of the Sahel Sultanates, who were totally dependent on the French colonial government and who feared that the PPT would consolidate Southern–Christian rule in an independent Chad.

In 1952, a new grouping appeared on Chad's political scene: Northerners inspired by pan-Arabism and pan-Islamism founded the *Parti Socialiste Indépendant du Chad* (PSIC). Their leader was Ahmad Koulamallah, a Baguirmi Arab and leader of the local Tijaniyya order. Although Koulamalla belonged to the Baguirmi aristocracy and to the rich Arab merchant class which had business connection with the Arab world, he held socialist views and identified himself with the ideology of Nasserism. He was regarded as the man of the Arab League in Chad.

At first, the new Northern grouping allied itself with the anti-colonial PPT against the colonial administration, French commercial interests and the traditional "stooges" of the French in the conservative UDT (AST). In 1957, a dramatic shift occurred in

Chadian politics. The PPT, which was part of the *Rassemblement Démocratique Africain* (RDA) of French colonial Africa, allied itself with sections of the conservative AST and abandoned its anti-colonial stance. The shift in the policies of the PPT corresponded to a similar shift of most RDA sections in French West and Equatorial Africa. In Chad the anti-colonial flag now passed to Koulamallah's supporters who founded the Muslim *Mouvement Socialiste Africain* (MSA), which replaced the PSIC and was opposed to the *Entente Republicaine* led by the former PPT. The French, who had opposed the PPT in the 1940s, transferred their support to the *Entente*. They had no permanent allies either in the North or in the South, but only an abiding interest in opposing the more radical anti-colonial nationalists and in strengthening the "moderates". In 1958, two years before independence, the conservative Muslims abandoned the *Entente* and formed with the MSA the *Union Socialiste Tchadienne* (UST). Thus, while in the early 1950s the anti-colonial Southern PPT was opposed by a conservative Northern UDT, in the late 1950s an increasingly conservative PPT was opposed by the whole Muslim North. After independence, a violent conflict, between the Southern government (supported by the French) and Muslim insurgents (supported mainly by Libya), raged in Chad for thirteen years (1965-1978). The front lines were fixed in the late 1950s, in the final days of decolonization,[8] when the country became polarised between a ruling Southern party and a Northern opposition party.

Chad became a sovereign state in 1960. Southerners dominated the government, the economy, and the army. The frustrated North attemptd to resist the *"Pax Sara"* in Chad by the formation of the *Parti National Africain* (PNA), which united all Northerners against the Sara dominated PPT. Francois Tombalbaye, the newly elected Prime Minister, adopted a *divide et impera* strategy between Northern conservatives and radical nationalists in order to effect the dissolution of the PNA. When he failed, he dissolved all opposition parties and transformed Chad into a single-party state ruled by the former PPT, which then became the *Union pour le progrès du Tchad* (UPT). From 1962 onwards, Tombalbaye established an oppressive political system. notorious for its corruption and brutality. In September 1963 all important Muslim leaders were imprisoned. Some survived long years of incarceration, while others were secretly liquidated. Again and again, the government was shaken by attempted *coupt d'états*, mutinies and assassination attempts, but with the help of the French security services and some good luck, Tombalbaye survived until 1975. In April 1975, he was killed while resisting a military takeover. Time and again Tombalbaye tried to break the isolation of his régime by initiating a reconciliation policy towards the Muslim North which had been in violent revolt since 1965. The movement of prominent Muslim opposition leaders from prison to ministerial positions and back to prison was a peculiar Chadian contribution to comparative politics.

Tombalbaye's regime was a Sara based, Southern dictatorship. This background explains the Muslim revolt which started in the Sahel in 1965. That revolt, and the ensuing civil war, led indirectly to Tombalbaye's fall in 1975, the defeat of the South in 1978-1979, and the Libyan invasion in 1980-1981. The paramount reason for the civil war, which raged in Chad in the 1960s and 1970s, between the Southern government and the Northern rebels, lies in the refusal of the Muslim North to accept as final the dramatic shift of power to the South in the colonial era.

The Northern Muslims regarded Southern rule as the continuation of colonialism with a black face. Not only were they ruled by the hated Saras after independence, but the French maintained French military rule in the B.E.T. until 1965. Later on, French troops were involved in the government's efforts to crush the revolt. Therefore, the Northern accusation that "the North remained colonised" made sense to the Muslim population. The rebel *Front Libération Nationale du Tchad* (FROLINAT), which fought against the Southern governments for more than twelve years, was founded in 1966 by urban, educated Northerners who were fiercely opposed to French colonialism and the Southern–Christian domination of Chad. FROLINAT regarded Tombalbaye's Chad as a neo-colony, dominated by capitalist French commercial interests, by the French army and security services, and by a collaborating Southern bourgeoisie. The young Northern students who led FROLINAT wanted the overthrow of the "puppet regime" and the withdrawal of the French troops, as well as the nationalization of foreign companies.

They were inspired by Nasser's doctrine of Arab Socialism and radical anti-colonialism. This ideological component of the in-

surgency was evidently important for Ibrahima Abatcha, the first
leader of FROLINAT.[9] Abatcha, a socialist and nationalist intellec-
tual from Kanem had led in 1958 the small, anti-colonialist *Union
Nationale Tchadienne* (UNT) which called on the population in
September 1958 to vote for independence and against Chad's
continued association with France in a plebiscite organised by
General De-Gaulle in the French African colonies. All other
political groupings in Chad — even Koulamallah's MSA —
supported the Gaullist proposals for autonomy within the French
community. The revolt by the North was not only an insurrection
against the South, but also a reaction to Tombalbaye's oppressive
rule, to the suppression of all opposition parties, and to the
imprisonment of all the leading Muslim opposition leaders in
September 1963.

The South fought bitterly to retain its dominance, because of
genuine fears that the North intended to restore the pre-colonial
slave raiding (called "*razzias*") were vivid in the South and
provoked a united Southern stand against a Northern takeover,
inspite of the fact that many people in the South (e.g. students and
intellectuals, Saras traditionally opposed to Tombalbaye's sub-
tribe and non-Sara ethnic minorities) had also suffered from
Tombalbaye's draconian government.

The Southerners could not dispense with the French, whom they
regarded as allies and protectors against a Northern takeover. The
vicious circle was complete: the North regarded Southern rule as
neo-colonial because of the French presence, while the South
remained allied with the French fearful of Northern power and
ambition. Both sides regarded the struggle as a matter of life or
death and the almost equal size of the population in the "Two
Chads" made it inconceivable for either side to accept defeat and
an inferior status.

The rebellion started in October 1965 among the Moubi
peasants in the Sahel zone, who revolted against the Sara tax
collectors. The brutal suppression of the uprising further incensed
the whole Muslim Sahel and the rebellion spread rapidly throughout the region. The government exacerbated the fury in the North
by imposing taxes on cattle and women, taxes designed to inflict
damage on the pastoral and polygamous Muslims of the North.[10]
In 1966, the Toubou tribesmen of the Saharan region joined the
rebellion under the spiritual leadership of the *derdé*, the traditional

ruler of the Teda-Toubou. For years the warlike Toubous were the backbone of the Northern guerilla forces under the military command of Hissen Habré (a French-educated lawyer from the Anakaza branch of the Daza-Toubou) and Goukouny Woddeye, the *derdé's* only son who survived the war against the government forces and their French allies.

Maladministration and the behaviour of the Southern security forces further inflamed the rebellion. The French administrators who had served in the North until independence had been highly qualified, fluent in Arabic and respectful of Northern traditions and sensitivities.[11] After independence, they were replaced by the less educated Saras who did not understand Arabic and who despised the North and its chiefs, religion, traditions, and values. The Sara governors were oppressive, corrupt and inefficient. They behaved as colonial rulers towards the people of the North, their implacable enemies and former slavers for hundreds of years. It was not coincidental that Sara tax-collectors, who, always accompanied by armed guards, used to extort taxes from the population ignited the first sparks for the conflagration. The army, composed wholly of Southerners (and some non-Muslim Hadjerai), took its historical revenge against the Northerners — their slavers in pre-colonial times. In one such episode in January 1965, a soldier was killed in a fight between locals and soldiers in a night club in the Northern town of Bardai. The army retaliated by forcing Toubou tribesmen to march naked through the streets and by imprisoning the entire male population. Harsh Southern rule in the North had precipitated the flight of the *derdé* to Libya in December 1966. His sons later became leading figures in the Northern insurrection.[12]

In addition to Northern aversion to Tombalbaye's oppressive rule and the neo-colonial character of his regime, the religious factor was a significant element in the revolt of the North. Although not all Muslims joined the rebellion, almost all those who did were Muslims. Their enemies were the Southern Christians and pagans, allied with the French infidels. Islam in Chad was orthodox, politicized and Arabised, and Chadian Muslims cultivated ties with Libya, Sudan and Egypt. Hundreds of Chadians studied at the al-Azhar University in Cairo, pan-Islamic and pan-Arab ideas were imported to Chad from Egypt by returning students, and by hundreds of thousands of Chadians who emigrated to Sudan and Libya, but who remained in touch with their home country. Radio Cairo and Radio Tripoli also contributed to the spreading of pan-Islamic and Arab nationalist ideologies in north Chad. The few Southerners among the rebels had to wear Muslim dress and to adopt Arab names in order to be accepted by the Muslim guerrillas. The Muslim insurrectionists recruited soldiers in the Muslim areas by emphasizing that the Chad government was composed of infidels who persecuted them.

While for FROLINAT, the major rebel organization, religious appeals were used to agitate against the government and to mobilize support among the Muslim peasants and nomads, religious extremists in the eastern Sahel spoke of founding a "Muslim dictatorship" and a "Muslim state where God's Book and the Envoy will reign". In the mid-1960s, an exile government of the "Muslim Republic of Chad" was founded in Khartoum by a rebel group which had links with the Sudanese Muslim Brotherhood. Islamic fundamentalism was also strong in the *Front Libération Tchadienne* (FLT) which refused to join the "secular" FROLINAT. There is no doubt that religious sentiments played a role in fomenting and spreading the rebellion and were also a significant factor in the ensuing Southern resistance. Chad's South saw itself as a Christian enclave surrounded by the Muslims of Chad's Sahel, Northern Nigeria and Cameroun.

Another cause of the revolt was the refusal of the government to recognize Arabic as the second official language to French. Thus, the Southern government denied an official status to the most widely spoken language in Chad. The Southerners did not regard Arabic as a national language because of its identification with the North and Islam. The Muslims resented the fact that in all public schools — including those in the Muslim North — the language of instruction was French. The Northern Arabophil students, who graduated from the private Arab College in Abéché and who studied in Sudanese and Egyptian universities, could not find employment in government and public service because they were not French educated. This counter-élite was well-represented in the leadership of FROLINAT whose declared aim was to make Arabic the first or second official language.

The grievances of the North were numerous and real. Economic discrimination certainly existed, and between 1960 and 1975 almost all government investments were concentrated in the

South. No serious efforts were made to close the educational gap between North and South. The drought in the early 1970s and the reluctance of the government to assist the starving population in the rebel stricken areas led to revolt.

All rebel organisations disavowed any separatist intentions and FROLINAT also emphasized its secular character. Its declared aim was not to detach the North, nor to impose Arab and Muslim rule in Chad. In its publications, FROLINAT represented itself as anti-colonial and patriotic. Its ideology and rhetoric were anti-colonial and nationalist but its base of support was regional, religious, and ethnic. Thus, despite FROLINAT's official pronouncements, the perception of the war as one between the Arabised Muslim North and the Christian-Pagan Sara South is a correct one.[13]

The Chadian civil war cannot be wholly understood without some reference to the French element in the complex equation. From 1960 to 1978, the French backed the Sara dominated governments, which were in general sympathetic to French interests and amenable to French influence. The North had opposed the French colonial occupation of Chad and resisted post-colonial French support to Tombalbaye's (1960-1975) and Malloum's (1975-1978) Southern governments. It is difficult to judge whom the Northerners hated more — the French who aided the Southerners or the Southerners whom they regarded as puppets of the French. In the 1960s and 1970s, the French maintained a military presence in Chad in the form of bases combat troops and advisers. The air bases of Fort Lamy (Ndjamena since 1973), Faya-Largeau and Mongo were of vital strategic importance for France. French troops and bombers were actively involved in the fighting against the Northern guerrillas, frustrating an early rebel victory in the late 1960s and early 1970s. Between 1968 and 1972, for example, units of the Foreign Legion did almost all the fighting in the Toubou areas of the North. In 1978, they established a *cordon sanitaire* around the capital. The French took care to avoid what they perceived as the danger of a Vietnam-like involvement that would have been costly and unpopular. Thus, they invested a lot of resources in building the Chadian army with the aim of confining the war to Chadian forces. French interests in Libya — which not only supported the rebels, but was also an important oil supplier of France and a vital market for the French armaments industry — were another important factor in French efforts in the 1970s, to limit its involvement and commitment to the Southern governments. French interests in Chad — the strategic significance of the air bases, the prospects of oil and uranium deposits and the political importance of Chad as a "domino" in the French sphere of influence in Africa — were balanced by its considerable economic interests in the Arab world and especially in Libya, the main patron of the Northern rebels.

II

LIBYA AND CHAD IN THE
PRE-QADHDHĀFĪ ERA

The interaction between Chad and Libya did not erupt suddenly with Mu'ammar Qadhdhāfī's rise to power. The entry of Libyan troops to Ndjamena in the latter half of 1980 had distant historical origins. Already in pre-colonial times, the major caravan routes from Chad led to the Libyan coast. For hundreds of years, intensive trade links connected Tripoli and Benghazi with Kanem, Baguirmi and Quaddai. The "white" Ouled Sliman Arab tribes from Libya were expelled in two waves from the Libyan Fezzan to Chad — in 1842 by the Ottomans and in 1928 by the Italians. Numerous Tripolitanian merchants settled in the commercial centres of pre-colonial and colonial Chad.[14] They played a key role in organizing, managing and financing the trans-Saharan slave trade in the 19th century. The Teda-Toubou of Tibesti also inhabited the southern Fezzan. For them the border had never existed.

The main link between Libya and Chad in the 19th and 20th centuries was provided by the Muslim *Sanūsiyya Order*. The Libyan based Sanūsiyya, which aimed to propagate Islam and to strengthen Muslim unity, expanded to northern and central Chad in the 19th century. The Sanūsis established *zāwiyas* all over the Saharan and Sahel regions. They served as military outposts, trade-centres, religious and missionary stations, and educational institutions.

Quaddai and the Teda-Toubou were allied with the Sanūsiyya in the 19th century. From 1899 to 1902, the Sanūsis' capital was Quru in North Chad.[15] The Sanūsis and their allies in Muslim Chad fiercely resisted the French conquest and pacification policy. The first major battle was in Bir Alali in 1902, and the main Sanūsi centre in Ain Galakka capitulated in 1913. The last Sanūsi *zāwiya* in Saharan Chad fell in 1920. Thus, for almost two decades, the Sanūsis resisted the French advance into Muslim Chad. Their most important allies in Chad were Chai, the *derdé* of the Toubou who finally fled to the Libyan Koufra, and Sultan Ali of Quaddai. It is interesting to note how current events are rooted in history: in the 1960s, Tibesti and Quaddai again became centres of rebellion with strong Libyan connections. In 1966, the *derdé* — this time Woddeye Kichidemi — again had to flee to Koufra.

The temptation of rulers in Libya to push southwards towards Lake Chad existed well before Qadhdhāfī's troops invaded Chad. In 1909-1910 the Ottoman Turks, who ruled Tripolitania until the Italian conquest, attempted to establish a presence in North Chad by fortifying Bardai. The capture of Tripoli and Benghazi by the Italians in 1911, however, forced the Ottoman troops to withdraw from Chad in order to resist the Italian invasion of Libya.[16]

In the Italian era (1911-1942) there were constant attempts to enlarge the Italian sphere of influence southwards. Libya was considered a potential base for the Italian penetration of Africa to Lake Chad and beyond. In 1951, Libya became an independent state led by a Sanūsiyya dynasty. King Idris Sanūsi of Libya demonstrated his interest in Chad. In 1954 Libyan motorized units attempted to occupy the Aouzou Strip in North Chad, but were repulsed by French troops. After Chad's independence and the outbreak of the Muslim rebellion, Libya provided the insurgents with bases in the Fezzan and with food, arms, money and passports.[17] In 1966, a group of Libyan soldiers of Chadian origin joined the rebellion. Another group which had come from Libya to join the rebels, consisted of students from the Islamic University of Beida. The Teda-Toubou, who played a crucial role in the rebel movement from 1966, had excellent relations with the Libyan Royal Court. From the beginning of the *derdé*'s exile in Libya (December 1966), Libya became the centre as well as the base and the sanctuary of the Toubou rebels. Relations between Idris Sanūsi and the Sahel rebels, particularly the "progressive" Abba Siddiq were much cooler and sometimes even hostile.

In 1969, when the Libyan King was deposed, observers expected relations between the government of Chad and Libya to improve because the rebels in Chad had enjoyed links with ther Sanūsi Royal Court. Qadhdhāfī's *coup d'état* did briefly sever the links between Libya and the Toubous in North Chad, and relations between Tombalbaye's Chad and Qadhdhāfī's Libya did in fact improve.[18] However, it soon became evident that Libya's state interests, Arab nationalism and Muslim solidarity, were pushing Qadhdhāfī to renew and even to increase significantly Libyan support to the Muslim insurgents in Chad: initially for Abba Siddiq's forces in the Sahel and, after 1971, for the Toubou forces in the Saharan North. It is known that a few hundred of Idris Sanūsi's royal guards were trained in guerilla warfare in Koufra and were sent by Qadhdhāfī into North Chad. It is ironic that when regular Libyan troops entered Chad in the 1970s, the anti-Libyan *Forces Armées du Nord* (FAN)˙ led by Habré termed the act a "Sanūsi invasion", despite the enmity harboured by Qadhdhāfī to the Sanūsis.

III

QADHDHĀFĪ'S ESCALATING INVOLVEMENT IN CHAD IN THE TOMBALBAYE PERIOD
(1969-1975)

Hundreds of years of Libyan connection with the "desert of deserts" to the south, the pan-Islamic zeal to consolidate Islamic political power under Libya's guidance in the Islamic Sahel belt of Black Africa, hopes to gain access to the important uranium deposits in Northern Chad (and in Niger as well) and ambitions to turn Libya into a major regional power proved to be stronger than Qadhdhāfī's aversion to the Sanūsiyya supporters in Chad.

Chad's cordial relations with Israel — dating back to the early days of independence — reinforced Qadhdhāfī's hostility toward Tombalbay's regime. The Libyan demand to expel the Israelis from Chad was persistently raised by Qadhdhāfī after his assumption of power in 1969. Libya officially accused Chad of harbouring Israeli bases, serving Israeli interests, and being subservient to "Zionist capital and influence which seeks to enslave Africa".[19] Tombalbaye was personally attacked as an ally and a puppet of Israel, who received orders from the Israeli ambassador.[20]

Since 1970 Qadhdhāfī's Libya had provided increasing political, financial, and military support for the Chadian Muslim insurgents. Under Qadhdhāfī the rebels received for the first time modern weapons to replace the outmoded Second World War guns used by the guerillas in the 1960s. In 1969 the first permanent base of FROLINAT was opened in Libya. Libyans, Palestinians and North Koreans instructed the Chadian insurgents. FROLINAT gradually became a semi-regular army frequently clad in Libyan uniforms. What was called "Ho-Chi Minh Trail" from the Libyan Koufra to Northern Chad assured FROLINAT a constant supply of modern weapons and freshly trained reinforcements.

In order to preserve its influence, Libya did everything possible to subvert Tombalbaye's recurrent efforts to reach a reconciliation with the *derdé* Woddeye Kichidemi and with Abba Siddiq — the leaders of the insurrections in the Saharan and Sahelian North. At that time Qadhdhāfī's Libya was also deeply involved in the internal politics of the rebel organizations. When, in 1971,

Chadian students in Libya revolted against FROLINAT leader Abba
Siddiq — whom they regarded as too conservative and an
"armchair revolutionary" — the Libyan government intervened
on behalf of Abba Siddiq by suspending scholarships of trouble-
some students. The Libyans also interfered in a clash between
Abba Siddiq and the exiled *derdé* who accused Siddiq's forces of
leaving behind wounded Toubou guerillas in Tibesti. Qadhdhāfī
put the *derdé* under house arrest and thus again tipped the scale in
Siddiq's favor.[21]

In August 1971, tension culminated between Tombalbaye's
Chad and Qadhdhāfī's Libya. On 27 August, an attempted *coup
d'état* against Tombalbaye's regime was foiled. The timing may
have been decided by Qadhdhāfī to prevent a reconciliation in
Chad. A possible indication of that is the fact that it occurred after
Muslim leaders like Jibril Khayrallah and Ahmad Koulamallah
had been freed from prison and after Muslim politicians had joined
the government. One of the captured conspirators reported that he
had been trained in Libya and that the aim of the coup was to
"regain Chad for the Muslims".[22]

Tombalbaye reacted furiously. The Libyan diplomats were
expelled from Fort Lamy, diplomatic relations were severed and
all aerial communications cut. Chad's President attacked the
"diabolical pretensions of President Qadhdhāfī" and his "religious
and racial fanaticism". He declared that Chad as a secular state
would oppose Qadhdhāfī's objective to "impose Islam on us". He
condemned Libya for following a racist policy and expelling the
Chadian community residing in Libya. Tombalbaye and Foreign
Minister Baba Hassne spoke about Libyan "imperialism". and
"expansionsim". Speakers in the National Assembly also voiced
their opposition to Chad becoming a Libyan "puppet-state" and
raised the spectre of a Libyan invasion.[23] Tombalbaye tried to
mobilize support for his policies in Black Africa by emphasizing
the contradictions between "white" Arab Africa and black
"African" Africa.

Chad also threatened to claim the Toubou inhabited Fezzan of
southern Libya in which Chad had "historical rights".[24] Tombalbaye went as far as offering Chadian territory as a base of
operations to Libyan exiles intent on toppling the Qadhdhāfī
regime.[25] Libya, on the other hand, accused Chad of suppressing
Islam and Muslims; of racial persecution against Arabs; of

discrimination against the Arab language and culture and of harbouring and training anti-Qadhdhāfī mercenaries. On 17 September 1971, Libya officially recognized FROLINAT as the "only legitimate representative of the people of Chad" and allowed it to open offices in Tripoli.[26]

Although Qadhdhāfī openly declared his support for the "armed struggle of the people of Chad"[27] he "never supported FROLINAT fully, clamping down on its activities if Libya's other interests were at stake".[28] In the spring of 1972, one of the recurrent, apparent reconciliations between Chad and Libya occurred. At that time French troops and bases remained in Chad, and Libya did not want to jeopardize the Mirages deal with France. Succumbing to French pressures and in accordance with a national *Realpolitik* Qadhdhāfī decided that the time was not propitious for Tombalbaye's downfall and for a pro-Libyan take-over in Chad. Therefore, on 17 April 1972, Libya resumed relations with Tombalbaye's government and promised to reduce its support for FROLINAT. The Chadian government realized that French interests in Libya and the French public's fear of a Vietnam-like French involvement in the civil war would not enable the French to launch an all out offensive to liquidate the rebellion. Therefore, in 17 April 1972, the situation was ripe for both sides to compromise and meet half-way — even if only for a tactical armistice. When resuming relations with Libya, Chad gave in to Libyan pressures to declare its support for "armed struggle of the Palestinian people".

In November 1971, another deal was struck between Tombalbaye and Qadhdhāfī. After French combat units had withdrawn from actual fighting on the government side in the summer of 1972, Tombalbaye saw no other way to appease Qadhdhāfī and to deflect the Libyan danger than by breaking diplomatic relations with Israel. Within days, after the break of relations on 28 November 1972, Tombalbaye paid a state visit to Tripoli, where he denounced Israel and Zionism as colonialist and aggressive, and declared Israel to be a threat to the security of Chad and the whole of Africa. Qadhdhāfī reciprocated by praising the "noble attitude of Chad towards the Zionist enemy". In recognition of his compliance Tombalbaye was promised $93,000,000 and a reduction of Libyan support for FROLINAT.

In addition to the break with Israel, Tombalbaye was forced to agree to the cession of the Aouzou Strip in Northern Chad to

Libya and to demonstrate his sympathetic attitude toward Islam. Tombalbaye appeared at Muslim ceremonies and festivities, sometimes in Muslim dress. Following his visit to Saudi Arabia, Radio Chad even called the Protestant Tombalbaye *al-Hajj* Tombalbaye. Chad also recognized the PLO and allowed it to open an office in Fort Lamy.[29] The "reconciliation" between Qadhdhāfī and Tombalbaye was crowned by a Treaty of Friendship signed in December 1972.

Tombalbaye's appeasement of Qadhdhāfī proved futile. Libyan promises for large-scale financial aid soon proved to be hollow. Although some money was channelled to Chad through the newly created *Banque Tchado-Arabe*, Chad did not receive the $93,000,000.[30] Libya continued to support FROLINAT almost unabatedly, though for a short while, a few FROLINAT bases in Libya were closed. Almost simultaneously with ther public demonstration of friendship between Chad and Libya, Abba Siddiq continued to use Radio Tripoli to call on the people of Chad to rise against Tombalbaye.

IV

LIBYA'S ANNEXATION OF THE AOUZOU STRIP

In April 1972, Qadhdhāfī ordered his troops to occupy the Aouzou Strip — 3,700 sqm of North Chad — containing rich uranium deposits.[31] The occupation of the Strip advanced the border between Chad and Libya two hundred miles southwards and was one of the first indications of Qadhdhāfī's territorial ambitions.

The Libyans built a *zāwiya*-like complex combining religious, educational and social institutions in the town of Aouzou. In addition, they built airfields, defended by SAM-missiles, and made preparations for exploiting the uranium, iron and phosphate deposits in the area.[32]

From 1973 onwards, Libyan maps showed the Aouzou Strip and chunks of territory from Niger and Algeria as being within the international boundaries of Libya.[33] With regard to the Aouzou Strip, Qadhdhāfī's Libya followed the policy of the deposed Sanūsi dynasty. Only the newly-acquired Libyan wealth and power made the difference between the failure of the 1950s and the success of 1970s.

Libyan claims to Aouzou were articulated as follows:

(1) that the colonial border between Chad and Libya, agreed upon by France and Britain in 1899, was illegal. The Libyans insisted that when France and Britain delimited their respective spheres of influence after the Fashoda incident, they needed the consent of Ottoman Turkey — then ruling today's Libya — to comply with international law. The Ottomans never consented. In Libyan eyes, the Ottoman presence in North Chad in 1910-1911 supports their claim;[34]

(2) that Libya has an historical and ethnic claim to the region as evidenced by the Sanūsi role in North Chad and the ethnic affinities of the Toubous on both sides of the border;

(3) that the Laval–Mussolini Rome Agreement of 1935, accorded to Libya the Aouzou Strip and other pieces of land in Niger and Algeria. The Rome Agreement had been negotiated in

order to fulfill promises made to Italy by Great Britain, France and Russia in the Treaty of London in April 1915 — i.e. a commitment to border changes in Erithrea, Somalia, and Libya in return for Italy's readiness to desert the Triple Alliance and to enter the First World War on the side of the *Entente;*[35]

(4) that Tombalbaye had recognized the legitimacy of the new border in 1972.[36] Tombalbaye very probabaly sold the Aouzou Strip to Libya in 1972, in exchange for promises to reduce support to FROLINAT and for badly needed financial aid.

The Libyan claims do not correspond to all historical facts. The Mussolini–Laval Agreement was never ratified by France, due to tensions which had emerged with Fascist Italy regarding the status and future of Tunisia. The Italian Foreign Minister Count Ciano confirmed in 1938 that the Agreement was null and void. In 1955, after Libya's independence, France and Libya signed a Friendship Treaty recognizing the 1899 colonial border. French forces continued to hold the Aouzou Strip after 1935, an indirect indication that the Italians did not assert the legal validity of the Rome Agreement. Almost all Chadian leaders — including General Malloum, who ruled Chad from 1975 to 1978, rebel leader Hissen Habré, who became Prime Minister in August 1978, and guerilla commander Goukouny Woddeye, who became President in 1979 — indicated their opposition to the Libyan annexation of Aouzou. They also denied the legality of Tombalbaye's "sell-out" of Aouzou,[37] and argued that the Libyan occupation not only violated the UN Charter, but also the 1964 Cairo OAU declaration which accentuated the sanctity and inviolability of the colonial borders in post-colonial Africa. In addition, Chad supported the 1899 British–French agreements for geographical reasons, because the 1899 border is a line drawn to the south of all major oases in the southern Libyan desert. Claims and counterclaims notwithstanding, Lybian troops had established their first bridgehead in Aouzou in 1972, nine years before they entered the gates of Ndjamena.

V

CONTINUING HOSTILITY AND TENSION:
Libya's Relations With Malloum's
Military Government
(1975-1978)

On 14 April 1975, Tombalbaye's fifteen years of dictatorship came
to an abrupt end. The army overthrew the government in a swift
coup d'état and assassinated President Tombalbaye. The former
Chief of Staff General Felix Malloum, who had been imprisoned
by Tombalbaye on charges of conspiracy, was freed and installed
as the new Head of State. The new rulers were high officers of
Southern Sara origin so that their *coup d'état* did not fundamental-
ly change the relations between a ruling South and a rebellious
North. The officers acted because Tombalbaye had violated their
corporate pride by publicly referring to the army as a "clique of
thiefs and robbers", by incarcerating officers who were not to his
liking, and by building up a rival Presidential Guard against the
eventuality of a military *coup d'état*. The repression during the
"Cultural Revolution",[38] the attempt to impose the pagan Sara
initiation rite called *Yondo* on Christian Saras and non-Saras; the
persecution of Christian missionaries and Church dignitaries in the
name of African nationalism and a return to the roots (*authentici-
té*) made Tombalbaye's rule unpopular even in the Christian
dominated South.[39] Rumours circulated that Tombalbaye intended to declare Chad an Empire and to crown himself Emperor
à la Bokassa.[40] His failure to provide relief for the victims of the
drought in the Sahel, and the unsuccessful war against FROLINAT
and the other Northern guerrillas were additional factors which
made the military *coup* possible and popular.

Libya recognized the new military government immediately,
probably for tactical reasons. However, FROLINAT promptly
branded the new régime as "Tombalbayism without Tombalbaye"
because the ruling generals were all from the Sara South. It
became clear, right from the beginning, that Malloum's government had a "hawkish" attitude toward Libya. The *coup* itself was
explained by the necessity to remove Tombalbaye for betraying

Chad by "selling" the Aouzou Strip to the Libyans.[41] Malloum's government insisted that Libyan encroachment in the Strip was illegal. Malloum himself vehemently attacked its formal annexation by Qadhdhāfī in 1976 and his government organised mass demonstrations against Libya's policies and the "diabolic ambitions of the régime in Tripoli".[42] It also called on the OAU to intervene against the violation of the OAU basic principle regarding the sanctity of the borders at the time of independence. The OAU summits in Libreville (July 1977) and Khartoum (July 1978) became battlegrounds for Libyans, who accused Chad of serving "French imperialism" and persecuting Libyan citizens in Chad, and Chad's representatives who accused Qadhdhāfī's Libya of fomenting separatism and coveting territory in North Chad.[43] The Chadian government talked about a Libyan conspiracy to found a Toubou client state by detaching chunks of territory from Chad, Niger, and Algeria.[44]

Massive Libyan support to the FROLINAT forces and especially to the *Inter-Army Council* (combining those groups under the command of FROLINAT's Second Army commander Goukouny Woddeye) continued throughout the Malloum era. Libyan policy was aimed at foiling the reconciliation policy — initially followed by Malloum — towards the Muslim North. In order to convince FROLINAT to give up its fight, the ruling *Conseil Supérieur Militaire* (CSM) coined the slogan "CSM — FROLINAT: même combat".[45] In 1975-1976 Malloum succeeded in winning over minor factions of the insurgent movement to his government. Woddeye Kichidemi, the *derdé* of the Toubous returned from his Libyan exile in December 1975 and declared his support for Malloum. The *derdé*'s son Goukouny Woddeye refused to follow in his father's footsteps and was encouraged in this by Qadhdhāfī. Both Goukouny and Qadhdhāfī regarded Malloum's gestures towards the Muslim North as tactical moves which would not change the basic character of the Malloum government from being Southern, Christian, Sara, pro-French and conservative. Malloum attacked Qadhdhāfī's "sadistic pleasure in undermining our reconciliation".[46] In April 1976, Qadhdhāfī tried to oust Malloum by supporting a mutiny. The coup and the planned assassination of Malloum failed and the Libyan-trained leader of the putsch was tried and executed.

Libyan involvement in Chad reached a high point in the summer of 1977. when FROLINAT's Second Army, supported by Libyan troops and armoured units, conquered most of the B.E.T. region, including the urban centres of Zouar, Bardai and Qunianga well south of the disputed Aouzou Strip. Radio Chad denounced the "Hitlerite ambition of the Colonel from Tripoli" who wanted to "destroy Chad and build an atomic bomb with the uranium from Aouzou".[47] Malloum spoke of the "growing appetite of the Libyan conquerors" and ordered the closure of the Chadian–Libyan Arab Bank, the Libyan Cultural Center, and all Libyan schools.[48]

At the same time the Egyptians became involved in Chad's dispute with Libya. A joint Egyptian–Sudanese delegation, headed by Egypt's Vice-President Ḥusni Mubārak, visited Chad and declared its support for the Chadian demand to open negotiations about the Aouzou Strip, which Libya regarded as a non-negotiable part of southern Libya. President Anwar al-Sādāt publicly voiced his support for Malloum, reflecting Egyptian and Sudanese fears of becoming encircled by a chain of radical and hostile states consisting of Libya, Chad, Ethiopia, and South Yemen. Egypt's and Sudan's stand, as well as cautious gestures of support for Malloum by other Arab conservative states such as Morocco and Saudi Arabia, demonstrated that not all Muslim states supported the rebellion of the Muslim North in Chad. Religious solidarity is only one of several factors in the attitude of states towards the civil war in Chad. Others, such as the radical-conservative cleavage in the Arab world and Africa, narrow state interests and global interests also played an important role.

Continuous Libyan attacks against Chad throughout 1977 led Malloum to break diplomatic relations with Libya on 6 February 1978. Chad also complained to the UN Security Council of Libya's aggression. Within a few days, however, Malloum had to withdraw his complaint and resumed diplomatic relations with Libya. Rapid Libyan military advances and the fall of B.E.T.'s capital Faya–Largeau into the hands of combined FROLINAT–Libyan troops on 19 February 1978, as well as the loss of almost half of Chad's army in the fighting compelled Malloum to try to save himself by appeasing the Libyans. From a position of political and military weakness, Malloum had to accept a Libyan invitation to the first

Sebha Conference (23-24 February 1978), which was attended by the Heads of States of Libya, Chad, Niger, and the Vice-President of Sudan.

A second conference took place in Sebha and Benghazi in early March. Then the Heads of States were joined by the three leaders of the Inter-Army Council led by Goukouny Woddeye. The result of these conferences were the Benghazi Accords which included the following main points:[49] (1) freedom for all political prisoners in Chad; (2) withdrawal of all French forces; (3) a formal recognition of FROLINAT; (4) an immediate cease-fire to be supervised by a military committee composed of officers from Niger and Libya; (5) the appointment of Niger, Sudan and Libya as guarantors of the agreement; (6) Libyan promises of financial aid to Chad and (7) a Libyan readiness to open negotiations on the border issue. All in all, the accords were imposed by Qadhdhāfī, revealing that nothing of political significance could happen in Chad without Libyan consent. The Benghazi Accords tacitly legitimized the Libyan military presence and institutionalized the Libyan involvement through Libya's dominant role in the military committee. They also supplied Libya with the rationale for any future large-scale invasion, fulfilling, as it were, its role as guarantor of the Benghazi Accords.

Qadhdhāfī's Sebha initiative raises the question of why Libya halted the march to the capital of its troops and those of its allies. Apparently, Libya gave in to strong French pressure in order not to risk a total breach with an important arms supplier. From a Libyan point of view it also served to demonstrate to Goukouny's forces their dependance on Libya. Negotiations with Malloum and an imposed cease-fire served this purpose excellently. The Benghazi Accords, which were supported by the Inter-Army Council, were also directed against the January 1978 Khartoum Agreement between Malloum's military government and Habré's FAN which had split from the main body of FROLINAT. That agreement was endangered because Habré had not been invited by Qadhdhāfī to join the Sebha conferences. Both Qadhdhāfī and Goukouny wished to create the impression of a Malloum–Goukouny deal in order to break the recent anti-Libyan Malloum–Habré alliance. The initiative might also have been a tactical Libyan ploy to irritate Malloum, to bring about a withdrawal of the French and to pave the way for a smooth victory by the

Libyan-backed forces, without a direct clash with the French military presence. The Sebha initiative was a shrewd translation of military successes into political advantages and demonstrated Qadhdhāfī's aptitude for *Realpolitik*.

The Benghazi Accords collapsed less than a month after they had been signed. In April 1978, the cease-fire broke down and Goukouny's forces advanced to within 100 miles of the capital. Only massive French intervention and the establishment of a *cordon sanitaire* around the capital by French troops prevented the fall of Malloum. FROLINAT accused the government of breaking the Benghazi Accords by not withdrawing the French troops. Malloum accused Libya and FROLINAT of acting in bad faith by increasing the military pressure and disregarding the cease-fire.[50] Libya strengthened the renewed offensive of FROLINAT with troops and logistical support. Goukouny's forces, pushing southwards, were commanded by Libyan officers and Libyan SAM-9 missiles were set up in Faya-Largeau in order to meet any French aerial attack.[51] In July 1978, the Libyans decided to reach an understanding with the French on a *de facto* partition of Chad into Libyan and French spheres of influence. Libya's Prime Minister 'Abd al-Salām Jallūd was dispatched to Paris for that purpose. The secret agreement with France established the 14th parallel as the dividing line between Libyan and French forces.[52] Chad became to all intents and purposes a Libyan–French condominion. Qadhdhāfī is said to have told the French: "if you leave me the Muslims, I will leave you the Blacks".[53] He spoke for the first time about the "Libyan" population of North Chad, thus preparing the ground for an ethnic-irredentist rationale for further expansion southwards. Libya also presented itself as a protector of Islam against the African and French infidels in the Muslim belt of Sahel states.

The Libyans were regarded as enemies of Chad not only by the government but also by a great part of the rebel forces. Hissen Habré, until 1976 the commander of FROLINAT's Second Army, was a sworn opponent of Libya, which he regarded as the "Enemy number one of Chad" because of its imperialist ambitions. Habré did not hesitate to talk about "the theory of an Islamic living space, a Qadhdhāfī version of the Hitlerite theory of living space".[54]

A document published in 1977 by Habré's FAN accused the Libyans of racism against blacks. The document tells about the fate of blacks in Libya, about discrimination in the Libyan army, about the persecution of black men who want to marry white Arab women and about the use of the term *abid* (slave) to describe blacks.[55] Habré resented the Libyan occupation of the Aouzou Strip and attacked Tombalbaye for weakness towards the Libyans. On this common anti-Libyan basis, rumours of a possible rapprochement between Habré and the Malloum government began to gain credibility. In June 1976, Habré's Second Army was engaged in heavy fighting around Oumchia against invading Libyan troops. Habré spoke of Qadhdhāfī's imperialism, and called the Libyans "another kind of whites who want to enslave us".[56] In October 1976 forces in FROLINAT — led by Habré's second in command Goukouny Woddeye — who regarded the Libyans as the lesser evil and who insisted that the paramount task was to overthrow the "neo-colonial" Malloum government deposed Habré.[57]

The deposed Habré was replaced by Goukouny. Habré was also expelled from the Second Army stationed in Tibesti and retreated with a few hundred Anakaza tribesmen to his Borkou stronghold. As indicated earlier the split was also a tribal one — the Teda–Toubou supported Goukouny while the Anakaza tribe of the Daza–Toubou provided Habré's base of support. Most of the fighting force remained with Goukouny who decided to make peace with Qadhdhāfī in order to concentrate all resources on removing Malloum. From then on FROLINAT's various factions could be classified according to their attitude toward Libya. The forces co-operating with Libya were FROLINAT's First Army, Second Army and remnants of the Vulcan Force. They formed the Inter-Army Council and accepted, at least for tactical and short-term reasons, the Libyan military involvement. The forces hostile to Libya were Habré's FAN, Abba Siddiq's FROLINAT-originel and Abū Bakr 'Abd al-Rahmān's Third Army operating in Kanem. The anti-Libyan forces were supported by Sudan, Saudi Arabia, Egypt and Nigeria. Thus the attitude to Libya became the dominant reason for the deep rifts developing within the Muslim North.

Libyan meddling in the affairs of the rebel forces began in 1971, when Libyan troops intervened in a revolt within FROLINAT which was aimed at replacing Abba Siddiq. In 1973, two commanders of FROLINAT's First Army were executed in Libya on charges of treason. In March 1977, the Libyans probably contrived the death of General El-Baghlani in Benghazi. El-Baghlani, the commander of the Vulcan Force operating in the eastern Sahel, was suspected of negotiating with Malloum. His elimination paved the way for the adhesion of the Vulcan Force to the pro-Libyan Inter-Army Council. Qadhdhāfī invited only the co-operative FROLINAT factions to Sebha and Benghazi in February–March 1978. Accordingly, the Benghazi Accords were rejected by the other rebel forces — most significantly by Habré's FAN.

VI

THE COLLAPSE OF SOUTHERN DOMINATION:
Libya and the Malloum-Habré Coalition
(August 1978–February 1979)

In January 1978, Malloum's government and Habré's FAN concluded the Khartoum Agreement which aimed to reconcile North and South through the formation of a government of national unity. Libyan military pressure, Qadhdhāfī's Sebha initiative and continuing negotiations between Malloum's and Goukouny's representatives postponed the establishment of the CSM — FAN coalition. Malloum's government was in a desperate military situation and was compelled to negotiate simultaneously with Habré, Goukouny and Qadhdhāfī in order to achieve the best terms. By the summer of 1978, Malloum had become disillusioned both with Qadhdhāfī and Goukouny. The Libyans broke the Benghazi Accords and continuously pushed their forces into the Chadian heartland. Goukouny's *conditio sine qua non* for a reconciliation with Malloum was a French withdrawal, something the vulnerable Malloum dared not accept. Thus, in August 1978, the formation of a coalition government with Habré's men, in compliance with the Khartoum Agreement, became the only viable option for the hardpressed Malloum.

The French, too, did their utmost to bring about the appointment of Habré as Prime Minister. They were deeply involved in the fighting between the army and the Libyans in the spring of 1978. In May 1978 only massive bombardment of Libyan convoys by the French air force stopped the Libyan army one hundred and fifty miles from Ndjamena. The French, who spent $2,000,000 a day to defend Ndjamena, struggled to extricate themselves from the Chadian quagmire by installing a Northern Muslim Prime Minister in Ndjamena. The French hoped that Habré would wield enough political support in the North and that Goukouny might also be lured finally into a Chadian nationalist "Grand Coalition". They hoped to stabilize the situation in Chad by a French–Libyan understanding about their respective spheres of influence. The overriding French aim was to protect the uranium fields in neighbouring Niger, a vital ingredient of the *force de frappe*. The Sudanese and the Saudis were also active in promoting the Malloum–Habré coalition. They feared a radical Chad under Qadhdhāfī's control and regarded Habré's FAN, which had good anti-colonial, Muslim and Northern credentials as the only force capable of resisting the Libyan penetration.[58]

On 29 August 1978, the Malloum–Habré coalition became a political reality. The "hawks" in Malloum's CSM led by Foreign Minister Abdelkader Kamougué, opposed what they regarded as surrender by the Southerners but the moderate majority supported Malloum. They regarded the CSM—FAN compromise as a lesser evil and the only alternative to a total victory by pro-Libyan forces. The new coalition was based on the principle of parity. Malloum became President and Habré Prime Minister. The *Forces Armées Tchadiennes* (FAT) and FAN had equal representation in the government and the military *Comité de Défence et Securité* (CDS). Arabic now became Chad's second official language and Muslim FAN guerrillas took over strategic positions in the government and the bureaucracy. The 29 August 1978 was the beginning of the end of Sara rule in post-colonial Chad.

The Libyans strenuously resisted the Malloum–Habré deal. They knew that the Muslim Habré was no less anti-Libyan than the Christian Malloum. They extended Habré the formal courtesy of sending a cable of congratulations while preparing the ground to depose him. Radio Tripoli called the Malloum–Habré coalition "colonial" and "fascist."[59] Habré had no illusions. Within days after assuming office he launched a fierce verbal attack on the Libyans, accusing them of expansionist aims and plans to annex the whole B.E.T. region and Kanem,[60] in addition to the Aouzou Strip.

Malloum did not abandon his hopes for uniting all Chadians in order to contain the Libyans. He, therefore, continued to negotiate with Goukouny about the formation of a broad anti-Libyan alliance. Qadhdhāfī feared that Goukouny might be tempted to join the coalition government. To prevent such an eventuality, he was put under house arrest in Sebha. In the meantime, Qadhdhāfī supported the build-up of a pro-Libyan faction of the rebel forces led by Asīl Ahmat, a black Arab from the Sahel Region who had been a member of the National

Assembly in the Tombalbaye era.

Fights broke out between the Toubous of Goukouny's Second Army and Arabs who had originally belonged to FROLINAT's First Army. The Arabs who were loyal to Asīl Ahmt were mainly from Arab tribes in the Sahel and Chadian ethnic Arabs who migrated to Libya.[61] In October 1978 the Libyans decided to support Asīl's ethnic Arabs in the rebel forces and backed them in clashes with Goukouny's Toubous. Goukouny escaped from his house arrest in December 1978 just in time to prevent a pro-Asīl coup in the Second Army.[62]

Goukouny strongly believed in the independence and integrity of Chad and was far from being a Libyan client even in the days of the Malloum–Habré coalition. The following excerpt from an interview granted to *Africa Report* indicated his attitude towards the Libyans (the interview was granted before his imprisonment):

> "We have not changed our position regarding the occupation of Aouzou. It is an occupation. Libya arrived there to destabilize our revolt following the agreement between Tombalbaye and Qadhdhāfī.... After this there were better relations between us and the Libyans. They now give us aid and a small amount of arms. Everyone thinks we have helped Libya in the occupation of Aouzou. In fact we have denounced it repeatedly. All Chadians know that Malloum's government lies when it says we support the Libyans. All Chadians know we are fighting for a just cause. If today we cede some territory to Libya, tomorrow maybe we will give some to Sudan and then what will be left for Chad?"[63]

In February 1979, the marriage of convenience between the conservative Malloum and the radical Habré ended in an acrimonious divorce. Mutual suspicion was the main cause. Malloum feared that Habré's flirtation with young pro-Soviet officers in the army, as well as the recruitment to the army of young Muslims and the growth of FAN as a military force could lead to a pro-Habré shift in the balance of power in their shaky coalition. Habré's insistence that the Prime Minister's powers were not dependent on the President's approval increased Malloum's suspicions. Malloum who was reluctant to jeopardize his own position, slowed down the integration of Habré's guerrillas into the army and gendarmerie. He also refused to free from prison some of Habré's men and kept close watch on his aides. Habré interpreted these measures as indicating Malloum's bad faith. He also suspected that Malloum's negotiations with Goukouny were aimed at replacing the Malloum–Habré coalition with a Malloum–Goukouny team.

When Habré decided to act against Malloum, the French supported him tacitly. They concluded that only an authentic Northern Muslim government unencumbered by associations with the Saras' *ancien regime* could save Chad from falling into radical hands. In February 1979, fighting broke out between Habré's guerrillas and Malloum's soldiers and gendarmes. Thousands of Saras were slaughtered in Ndjamena by Habré's FAN. In the Southern town of Moundou one thousand Muslims were killed in anti-Northern riots. Tens of thousands of Saras left Ndjamena in the Muslim Sahel and returned to the safety of Sara territory in the South. Almost the entire bureaucracy, which was largely Sara, moved from Ndjamena to Moundou and Sarh in the South, thus stripping any future central government of the means to establish effective control in the whole of Chad. By the end of February 1979, FAN had driven the regular army, and the gendarmerie out of the capital. Habré became the only ruler in Ndjamena but not for long. Goukouny's Second Army, now called *Forces Armées Populaires* (FAP), exploited to the full the opportunity which the war between Malloum's and Habré's forces provided. Goukouny advanced his forces deep into the Sahel and on 23 March the first FAP soldiers entered the capital. With Libyan help Asīl's newly founded *Conseil Démocratique de la Révolution* (CDR), occupied strategic positions in the eastern Sahel. The Southern forces retreated to Sara country determined to defend their ethnic homeland. Malloum lost all power in the South and left the country. Kamougué, the Southern "hawk" who had attacked the Khartoum Agreement as appeasement of the North and who commanded the gendarmerie in the battle with Habré's guerrillas, now became the "Sara Lion", the crowned leader of the Saras.

By March 1979, four centres of power had emerged in Chad: Goukouny's FAP in the B.E.T. region and the central and western Sahel, Habré's FAN in the capital, the eastern Sahel and the north-east, Asīl's CDR in the eastern Sahel and Kamougue's FAT in the South. A fifth minot centre of power comrpised the *Forces*

Armées de l'Occident (FAO) based in Kanem. From the Libyan point of view, Asīl was their staunchest ally while Habré was their most notorious enemy. As subsequent developments demonstrated, Goukouny's FAP and Kamougué's FAT were the decisive forces in the confrontation between Qadhdhāfī's allies and enemies. Already in March 1979 the dividing line had become one between pro- and anti-Libyan forces rather than between North and South.

VII

THE MUSLIM NORTH TURNS AGAINST QADHDHĀFĪ:
The Goukouny–Habré Coalition
(March 1979–March 1980)

The breakup of the Malloum–Habré coalition in February 1979 and the entrance of Goukouny's forces into Ndjamena accelerated the power struggle between Goukouny's and Habré's forces. To prevent the clash between FAP and FAN — both basically nationalist and hostile to the Libyans — France and Nigeria pressured the archenemies to share power, thus to prevent a Libyan takeover. For this purpose, Nigeria invited the various forces to the first Kano Conference in March 1979. The Chadian participants — FAP, FAN, a Southern minority faction and the Kanem based *Mouvement pour la Libération du Tchad* (MPLT) — decided in Kano to form the *Gouvernement d'Union Nationale de Transition* (GUNT). Lol Mahamat Shawa (MPLT) became Prime Minister and the Southern Negué Djogo, deputy Prime Minister. However, real power was invested in the hands of Goukouny who became Minister of the Interior, and Habré, who took the defense portfolio.

The opposition to GUNT was led by Asīl's Arabs and Kamougué's Southerners. In June 1979, Asīl's CDR combined with other mainly Arab groupings such as Mahamat Abba's *Forces de Libération Populaire* (FLP), Abdalhi Adoum Dana's Vulcan Force and Abba Siddiq's FROLINAT — originel to form the *Front d'Action Commune Provisoire* (FACP). FACP was essentially an Arab alliance, while Goukouny's FAP and Habré's FAN were largely Toubou. In addition to FACP, GUNT was opposed by Kamougué's Southern forces (FAT). For Kamougué, any coalition with Habré, the man who had brought about his fall from the government in August 1978, who had expelled the Southern army from the capital and had slaughtered thousands of Saras in February 1979, was out of the question.

In the spring of 1979, Kamougué was toying with the idea of a Southern secession from Chad. Libya vehemently denounced

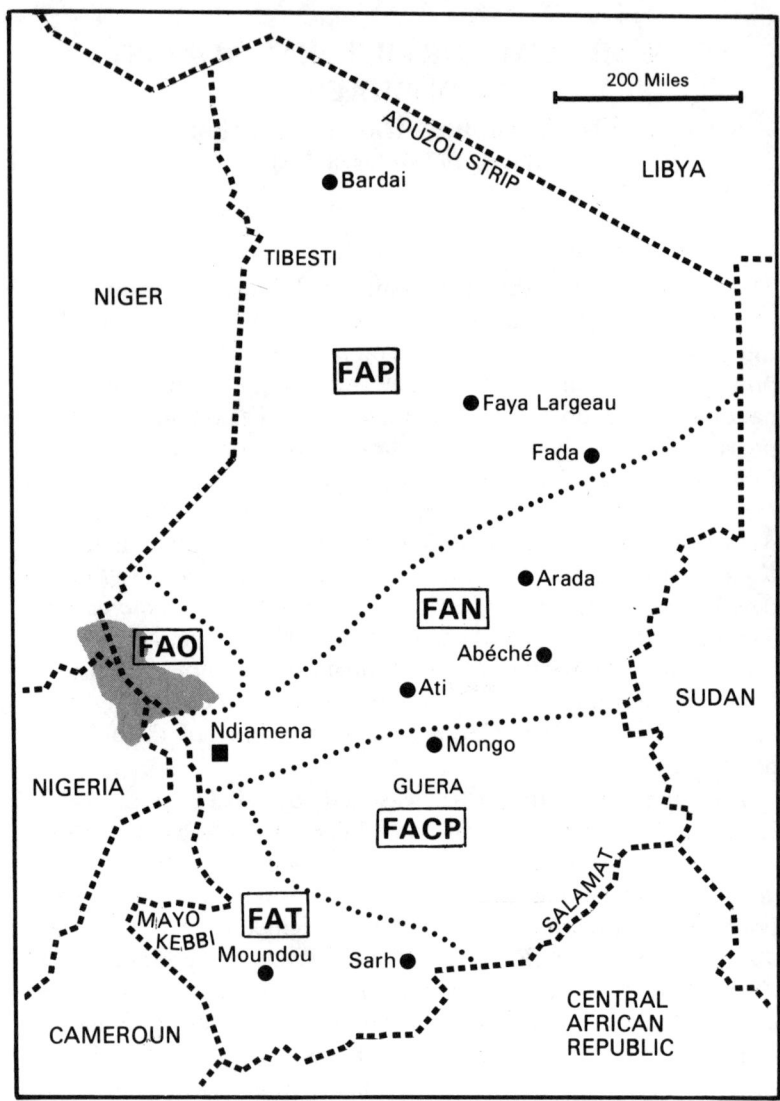

Map No. 2: The Big Five and their Areas of Operation

GUNT as the "Ndjamena gang", the "illegal fake alliance", and as being "pro-Israeli", "fascist" and "colonial".[64] Radio Tripoli attacked the "tribalism" and "fanatic tribal stands" of GUNT,[65] thus referring to Goukouny's and Habré's Toubou origins, as contrasted with Asil's Libyan supported Arabs. Qadhdhāfī understood that the only rationale of the Habré–Goukouny coalition was to block the Libyans and their clients. Jallūd, second only to Qadhdhāfī in Libya, arrogantly declared that "any arrangement in Chad which we will not approve will collapse".[66]

At the second Kano Conference in April 1979, the Libyans threatened to topple GUNT if the pro-Libyan groups were not invited to join the government. Nigeria, which desired to see a stable and independent Chad, decided to appease the Libyans by supporting their demand for a broad-based government. Goukouny and Habré detested Asil, Mahamat Abba and Dana, regarding them as "Libyan puppets".[67] Habré and Goukouny were put under house-arrest in Kano before they gave in to Libyan–Nigerian pressure to enlarge GUNT by adding the pro-Libyan factions. Back home, Goukouny and Habré, who had been incensed by their treatment in Kano, disregarded the Kano Agreement and the pro-Libyans remained out in the cold.

Qadhdhāfī reacted swiftly and brutally to GUNT's refusal to heed his pressures. Between April and August 1979, Libyan armoured units and thousands of Libyan soldiers advanced deep into Chadian territory. Fierce battles raged between Goukouny's forces and Libyan troops in Tibesti.[68] Already in April 1979, immediately after the formation of GUNT, Goukouny declared that the "war against Qadhdhāfī is a duty for every Chadian".[69] On 1 July 1979, Prime Minister Shawa called upon all Chadians to fight the Libyan intruders.[70]

GUNT appealed to the world against the "Libyan aggression" and even called on France to leave its forces in Chad. As a matter of fact, the French military mission and especially the French reconnaissance planes and bombers, provided vital assitance to the government's forces. The intruding Libyan troops and their allies were beaten by FAP and FAN forces, and Radio Ndjamena could celebrate the defeat of the Libyans known for their "arrogance" and "Machiavellism".[71]

Nor did Qadhdhāfī have any moral or religious scruples in supporting Kamougué's Christian FAT, which fought the Muslim

FAP and FAN. In May 1979 Kamougué — the Sara "hawk" known for his brutal treatment of Muslims — was welcomed in Tripoli by the Muslim fundamentalist ruler of Libya and concluded an alliance with him. Since May 1979, Libyan transport planes had delivered to the Southern capital Moundou weapons, ammunition and supplies for FAT.[72] Thus, in the spring of 1979, a strange realignment emerged in Chad: Libya supported the Southern Christians while France backed GUNT — the Northern Muslim Government.

Qadhdhāfī organized an international boycott of GUNT for not fulfilling the stipulation in the Kano Agreement to include all Chadian factions in the government. GUNT's representatives were actually expelled from the summits of the African Francophone States (Kigali/Rwanda — May 1979) and the Organisation of African Unity (Monrovia/Liberia — July 1979).

Goukouny's and Habré's refusal to include Qadhdhāfī's collaborators in their government was opposed not only by Libya, but also by Chad's other neighbours — Nigeria, Niger, Sudan, Cameroun and the Central Afridan Republic. Though fearful of Qadhdhāfī's ambitions, these states, nevertheless, thought it prudent to appease him. Their leaders assumed that by heeding his demands Goukouny and Habré would remain in control and avert an all-out attack by Asīl's and Qadhdhāfī's troops. In fact Chad's neighbours and all the anti-GUNT factions convened in Lagos on 26-27 May 1979 and brought pressure to bear on GUNT to enlarge its ranks.

In August 1979 the continuous military, political and diplomatic pressure forced GUNT to capitulate. In the second Lagos Conference held from 14-21 August 1979, Goukouny and Habré agreed to invite Libya's allies to the government. GUNT II, formed in November 1979, included five FACP ministers, among them Asīl as Foreign Minister and Mahamat Abba as Minister of the Interior. Goukouny became President, Kamougué Vice-President and Habré retained the defense portfolio. GUNT I (April 1979–November 1979) had been a truly Chadian, Northern-led, nationalist government. GUNT II contained the pro-Libyan members who were bound to collide with the anti-Libyan Habré. In early 1980, the FACP Ministers allied themselves with Goukouny's FAP, thus isolating Habré's FAN, and preparing the stage for Qadhdhāfī's creeping annexation of Chad into Libya's sphere of influence.

ORGANISATIONS AND LEADERS FORMING GUNT I AND GUNT II[73]

Organisation	Ethnic Base	Area of Operation	Leader	Attitude toward Libya	Participation in Government
1. Forces Armées Populaires (FAP)	Teda–Toubou	B.E.T. and Sahel	Goukouny	fluctuating	GUNT I, II
2. Forces Armées du Nord (FAN)	Anakaza	B.E.T. and Sahel	Habré	hostile	GUNT I, II
3. Mouvement pour la Libération du Chad (MPLT)	Kanembou	Kanem	Medela	hostile	GUNT I, II
5. Forces Armées Tchadiennes (FAT–Djogo)	Sara	South	Djogo	hostile	GUNT I, II
5. Forces Armées Tchadiennes (FAT–Kamougué)	Sara	South	Kamougué	fluctuating	GUNT II
6. Conseil Démocratique de la Révolution (CDR)	Arab	Sahel	Asil	supportive	GUNT II
7. Forces de Libération Populaire (FLP) — Front d'Action Commune Provisoire (FACP)	Arab	Sahel	Mahamat Abba	supportive	GUNT II
8. Vulcan Force — (FACP)	Arab	Sahel	Dana	supportive	GUNT II
9. Forces Armées de l'Occident (FAO)	Kanembou	Kanem	Abd al-Rahmān	supportive	GUNT II
10. FROLINAT originel	Arab	Sahel	Siddiq	fluctuating	GUNT II
11. FROLINAT fondamental	Massalit	Sahel	Hadjero Sanūsi	fluctuating	GUNT II

VIII

THE GOUKOUNY–HABRÉ CIVIL WAR AND THE LIBYAN OCCUPATION OF CHAD
(March 1980–December 1980)

In early 1980, mounting tension between the pro-Libyan FACP and the anti-Libyan FAN made the survival of GUNT II impossible. Intense battles were fought between FACP and FAN in the eastern Sahel, each of which regarded the area as its own political base. Libya strengthened FACP's position by a steady flow of arms and supplies. FACP grew in military and political stature inspite of the fact that its ethnic and regional base of support was quite narrow. At the same time Libya and FACP attempted to bribe FAN commanders and soldiers in order to win them over to their side. Qadhdhāfī and Asīl pressured Goukouny to get rid of Habré and to expel the French forces which were sympathetic to him. FACP ministers Asīl, Mahamat Abba and Dana threatened to topple GUNT II if Goukouny would not side with them in their struggle against FAN.[74] The ministers siding with Habré demanded an end to "Libya's international terrorism"[75] and the closure of the Libyan embassy.[76] Goukouny regarded both Habré and Asīl as enemies, but the Damocles Sword of Libyan power convinced him to side with Asīl.[77] Once again the pragmatic and flexible Goukouny became Qadhdhāfī's ally in Chad. The civil war between Habré's FAN and Goukouny's FAP began in March 1980. On 25 April 1980 Goukouny formally sacked Habré and his supporters from the government. Among the dismissed ministers were Finance Minister Mahamat Salah and former FACP minister Hadjero Sanūsi who had abadoned the "Tripoli Group" (FACP) and had denounced the Libyan aims to annex parts of Chad.[78] Goukouny's FAP commanded by the Libyan officer Mansur 'Abd al-'Azīz,[79] joined FACP in fighting Habré's troops. Kamougué also lost no opportunity to participate in the efforts to liquidate his arch-enemy Habré.

From March 20 battles were fought in and around Ndjamena. Thousands of soldiers were killed on both sides. In the French military hospital at Kousseri the wounded of both sides continued to fight each other,[80] and 100,000 refugees crossed the Chari River to Cameroun. Ndjamena was almost totally destroyed by artillery duels which continued throughout 1980.

The French forces (in the best tradition of the colonial *divide et impera*) supplied arms to both FAT and FAN. On 4 May 1980, Goukouny expelled the French forces, thereby putting an abrupt end to almost eighty years of French military presence. Although FAN's situation became more difficult after the French withdrawal it continued the struggle with the FAT–FAP–FACP coalition, helped by Egyptian and Sudanese supplies which reached Chad through the north-east.[81] FAN proved to be such an excellent fighting force that the FAT–FAP–FACP coalition had to appeal to the Libyan army for help.

GUNT sent a delegation to Tripoli requesting a Libyan intervention.[82] The Libyans responded enthusiastically. For years they were deeply involved in the affairs of Chad and built up Asīl's CDR (FACP) force. In April 1980 the first CDR units entered Ndjamena in Libyan uniforms. The Libyans treated the B.E.T. region as if it were already a part of Libya: they built air-bases there, issued Libyan identity cards to the population and introduced Libyan currency. In the South Libya maintained its support of Kamougué's forces.[83] Libyan transport planes and helicopters transferred 3,000 FAT soldiers from the South to Ndjamena on 18 October 1980 to join the battle against Habré.[84]

In October 1980 the Libyans did not conceal their intention to send their forces openly and officially into Chad. The Libyan Foreign Secretariat affirmed "that any attempt to keep out the states neighbouring Chad [Libya] is nothing but a conspiracy whose aim is continuation of the rebellion [by Habré]."[85] Radio Tripoli declared that "Libya would do all possible to establish peace in Chad if asked to do so officially".[86] In June 1980, a Treaty of Friendship was forced on Goukouny. This Treaty was to all intents and purposes a military pact legitimizing any Libyan involvement in Chad. In the same month the first 200 Libyan soldiers participated in the fighting in Ndjamena.[87]

Large-scale Libyan preparations were observed by American spy satellites in August 1980.[88] Sebha, in the Fezzan, became the major assembly base for the Libyan forces. Supply convoys, tank units and troops were sent from there to the Chadian battlefield.[89] In Chad the Libyans also took over bases and air-fields which had been vacated by the French forces. Dougia, a former French base 40 miles from Ndjamena, became in November 1980 the major Libyan base of operations. On 8 December 1980 the final onslaught on Ndjamena by the Libyans and their allies began. The Libyans committed 200 T54 and T55 tanks to the battle, and on 15 December 1980, Libyan tanks rolled into Ndjamena.

IX

THE LIBYA-CHAD UNION PROJECT

On 6 January 1981, the international community was stunned by reports from Tripoli about an impending merger between Libya and Chad. Many observers regarded the term "unification" as a euphemism for the annexation of a helpless Chad by the armed forces of Qadhdhāfī's Libya. The communiqué about unification (see appendix) which was published in Tripoli on 6 January 1981, following a state visit by Goukouny, spoke about open borders, the "unity of the masses and the resources", the obligation to assist each other in case of external aggression by a third party, and, most importantly, about the vision of one people's republic (*Jamāhiriyya*) uniting Libya and Chad.

According to various reports, Goukouny resisted the Libyan demands for a voluntary merger but he finally succumbed to brutal threats and pressures. There were rumours that the Libyans threatened to execute Goukouny if he did not agree to their plan and strong indications that Goukouny did not sign the Libyan–Chadian commuhiqué of his own free will. The Chadian delegation, headed by Goukouny, also included the Minister of the Interior Mahamat Abba (FLP/FACP) the Minister of Agriculture Lossinian Naimbaye (FAT) and the Minister of Education Mai Tchari Assounon (FAO). Foreign Minister Asīl (CDR/FACP) joined the talks only in the final stage. With the exception of Asīl, all the ministers refused to co-operate with the Libyans. Even the FACP-minister Mahamt Abba abandoned his former pro-Libyan stand and disassociated himself fronı Asīl. Upon his return to Chad, Naimbaye declared that "one day the Libyan units will have to leave Chad". The fact that the state visit was extended by two days and that "unification" was only announced at the last moment, indicates that Goukouny tried hard to resist the forceful Libyan tactics.[90]

The December 1980 headline of the official Libyan *Jamahiria Review* "No evidence of Libyan forces in Chad"[91] stood in sharp contrast to events in Chad and casts doubt on the credibility of the official Libyan pronouncements. Nevertheless, it is important to analyse the Libyans' explanation of their military presence in Chad (which after "unification" was no longer denied). Libya argued on legal grounds that the "Treaty of Friendship" of June 1980 entitled it to intervene at the request of Goukouny's legitimate government. In addition, the Libyans emphasized the basic right of sovereign states to unite. According to the Libyans this "right to unite" has a special significance in Africa, where the OAU recognized the "sacred right" of African peoples to establish unity and overcome disunity.[92] Security arguments were also mobilized to defend the Libyan actions. Libya argued that "Chad's security is linked to Libyan security". Qadhdhāfī's spokesmen stressed that "events in Chad have direct bearing on us because of our undeniable closeness to the country".[93] Libya even talked about Chad as a "vital living space".[94] The contention that Egyptian troops were involved on the side of FAN in the Habré-Goukouny civil war and that the Americans and French meddled in Chad, a state bordering Libya, was made to give credibility to the Libyan preoccupation with security. On a different tack, the Libyans cited the historical, geographical and ethnic ties between Libya and Chad to prove that they belonged to one family and that the colonial border was artificial and irrelevant.[95]

The reaction in Chad to "unification" was one of shock and dismay. Libyan tanks did not inhibit the Muslim people of Ndjamena from staging a demonstration against the union. Chadian students abroad protested against the merger.[96] The Saras threatened to secede from Chad. Kamougué, who had received Libyan aid throughout 1979-1980, defined the union as an "impossible marriage". He declared his strong opposition to the transformation of Chad into a Muslim State and warned that "Negro-Africa" would not accept any form of Arab rule. He defined all Chadians as "African Negroes" and the Libyans as "African Arabs" and insisted that "not one Chadian from the North to the South could accept this merger."[97] The Minister of Information Yantoingar Mairo Salomon declared bluntly that "we have a French history and culture and we are not going to throw all that away."[98] Siddiq, the doyen of the Northern Muslim struggle in Chad denounced the scheme as "annexation" and not "unification".[99] Jeune Afrique quoted a Muslim merchant from Kanem as saying that "even the dogs in Chad oppose unification".[100]

The Libyan move was received with anger and revulsion, not only in Chad, but in the whole of Africa. By the end of January 1981, Ghana, Mali, Niger, Upper Volta, Kenya, Nigeria, Sudan, Mauritania, Senegal, Gabon and the Central Afridan Republic had closed the Libyan embassies, expelled the Libyan diplomats or had even broken official relations with Tripoli.[101] Some had done so as early as 1980 because of Libyan subversion. African leaders of various political and ideological colorations denounced the Libyan moves.

Omar Bongo of Gabon charged the Libyans with "imperialism", Siaka Stevens of Sierra Leone attacked the "illegal invasion and occupation"; Seyni Kountché of Niger called on his countrymen to unite against the "Libyan danger", and even the radical Sekou Touré of Guinea condemned, in a joint declaration with Cameroun's Ahmadu Ahidjo, Libyan "expansionsim" and "hegemonism".[102] At the Islamic Summit in Tā'if, Niger's Foreign Minister Dawda Diallo attacked the Libyan misuse of Arabism and pan-Islamism.[103] In Niger, popular mass demonstrations against the Libyans took place in Niamey and Zinder, while in Nigeria some junior ministers and newspapers called for a Nigerian military intervention.[104]

The OAU committee on Chad — composed of twelve African states — hastily convened in Lomé (Togo) on 14 January 1981 and declared the merger illegal. The committee called on Libya immediately to withdraw its troops from Chad. Even the radical states (Guinea, Benin, Congo) which had supported the Libyan policy until December 1980, defended neither the unification nor Libya's military intervention in Chad. Libya's Foreign Minister Ali 'Abd al-Salam Turaykī fought a hopeless battle against the Lomé Resolution.[105]

African states also undertook some practical steps reflecting their concern and fear. Following urgent calls for help from the Central Afridan Republic and Niger, French paratroopers were flown to these countries. The Sudanese, who feared to becoming Qadhdhāfī's next victims, arranged hastily for a French military mission to visit Khartoum on 12 January 1981. Sudan also dispatched forces to the Chadian border, and Nigeria sent its fourth infantry division to the vulnerable Bornu region in the north-east. Military co-operation was also strengthened between African states. Egypt supplied arms to Gabon and Ghana,[106] while

Senegalese units entered Gambia twice in 1981 to foil a pro-Libyan *putsch*. In early 1981, black Africa was unusually united, the bond was opposition to Qadhdhāfī's schemes. The overall picture was one of hostility and panic. Muslim and Christian states, conservative and radical governments, Libya's neighbours in the Sahel and even states far away from the scene of action — all of them joined in condemning the Libyans. Ironically, the only state publicly to defend the fundamentalist Muslim Qadhdhāfī was the Christian Mengistu Haile Marriam, the radical leader of Ethiopia.

The furious African reaction was not without effect on Libyan policy. Within days the Libyans went back on the unification project. Already on 9 January 1981, they declared their willingness to honour the Lagos Agreements (which called for free elections in Chad and were difficult to reconcile with annexation). On 14 January Libya's Foreign Minister declared at Lomé that it was a mistake to talk about a "merger" between Libya and Chad. On 15 January, Qadhdhāfī declared that the Chadian–Libyan agreement called only for "unity of the two peoples" and open borders and not for inter-state amalgamation.[107] He denied allegations that Libya had "annexed" Chad and reiterated his commitment to "honour the freedom and independence of Chad."

On the other hand, he insisted on "full unity" between Chad and Libya and cited the European Economic Community as a model for such "full unity". In its February issue the *Jamahiriya Review* also defined the Libya–Chad Union as a "unity of the people" and not a "political unity as constitutionally known".[108] These vague and ambivalent declarations, together with Libyan assurances that its troops would withdraw from Chad, once peace and stability were secured there and when the French had withdrawn from the Central Afridan Republic, manifest Libya's retreat from "unification". In June 1981, Qadhdhāfī publicly agreed to withdraw from Chad should he be asked to do so by President Goukouny.[109]

Nevertheless Libya's insistence on "unity of the peoples", "full unity" and "open borders" left the door open for a creeping *de facto* annexation or, at least, the creation of a Libyan sphere of influence.

The Chadian government which was forced to accept "unification" against its will and better judgement tacitly welcomed the African reaction which helped it extricate itself gradually from the

Libyans. GUNT immediately issued a statement to the effect that the Goukouny–Jallūd Communiqué was only an informal declaration lacking legal validity.[110] The Chadian official news agency immediately published the Lomé communiqué thus suggesting that it supported the OAU stand on the Libyan invasion and unification.[111] Chadian leaders also attempted to play with words, saying that Goukouny had concluded an "alliance" but had not agreed to any "merger". Goukouny himself attempted to mobilize Nigeria as a counterweight to Libya. On a state visit in Lagos, he reiterated his adherence to the "integrity, unity and sovereignty of Chad." He dropped hints to his Nigerian hosts that "unification" had been forced on him, that he could not declare it null and void, but that the last word had not yet been spoken.[112] Within a week after "unification", Goukouny said on Radio Paris "Chad is Chad and Libya is Libya"[113], thus again, indirectly disassociating himself from the "unification" which he had been constrained to sign. In March 1981, Goukouny had already the courage to declare publicly that there was no union and that the Libyan army would withdraw.[114]

In GUNT the Southerners (Kamougué and Naimbaye) vehemently opposed the Libyan moves. *Le Matin* quoted Southerners saying "we only asked the Libyans for equipment and they sent their soldiers".[115] Ministers belonging to Goukouny's faction and even some of the former collaborators with Libya also declared their opposition to the merger. In a pro-Libyan Chad they could hold the reigns of power, in a Chad which would have become a remote province of Libya, they would sink into obscurity. Asīl and his supporters in the government must have felt that popular feeling ran high against the Libyans. The Minister of the Interior Mahammat Abba, a leading figure in the Tripoli Group, declared categorically that there would be no merger saying that the turmoil was rooted in an erroneous translation of the Goukouny–Jallūd communiqué. Still, he felt the need to pay lip-service to the "natural unity" and the "ties of blood" between Libya and Chad.[116] Even Asīl, who for years had carried Qadhdhāfī's flag in Chad and still remained "their man", stated in *"Al-mujāhid"* that "what was hastily interpreted as a merger is in fact a communiqué about the strengthening of relations between the two countries".[117] Thus, not even one Chadian leader fully endorsed the creation of "one Jamahiriyya" as had originally been announced.

The months that followed unification showed that the Libyans were facing stiff resistance in Chad — both in the form of defiance from the government and overt resistance from Habré and other opposition forces. In April 1981, there were violent clashes around Abéché between Libyan army units, supported by Asīl's forces, and Goukouny's army. Even Mahamat Abba's faction, which had been an integral part of Asīl's FAC[118] in 1979-1980 and hence was regarded as pro-Libyan, fought now on Goukouny's side against Asīl's and Qadhdhāfī's forces. The Tripoli government had to dismiss the commanders of the Abéché garrison in order to prevent a total break with Goukouny's GUNT.[119]

On 19 October 1981 fighting between Asīl's CDR and Mahamat Abba's FPL again broke out in the eastern Sahel.[120] From January 1981 Goukouny had been busily strenghening his political position and building a strong military force aimed at deterring Asīl and his Libyan patrons from staging a pro-Libyan coup. With this purpose in mind Goukouny attempted to dissolve the separate forces of his coalition partners and to integrate them in the newly created *Armée Nationale Intégrée* (ANI). Goukouny's overt explanation was that the move was intended to protect the "national independence" and "territorial integrity" of Chad.[121] ANI was put under the command of Col. Allafi, a Southerner and a former aide of Kamougué. The fact that Goukouny decided to make the anti-Libyan, Southern FAT the base on which ANI was to be built indicates that ANI's build-up was directed agasinst the Libyans. A gathering of FAP, FAT, FAO and FAC decided on 2 June 1981, that the Libyans would have to withdraw and be replaced by a neutral African force. Until then there was a need "to control the Libyan presence".[122] In July 1981 Adoum Togoi, a new Defense Minister with an anti-Libyan past, was named. It is also significant that Nigeria, Cameroun and Mitterand's France gave overt and covert support to Goukouny, hoping that he would ultimately turn against his Libyan allies. In the autumn of 1981 these hopes began to materialize, and in September Goukouny categorically rejected a new union scheme proposed by Qadhdhāfī.[123] In October Goukouny decided in favour of a *rapprochement* with France — GUNT decided to stay in the Franc zone, to consider a return to the Francophone UDEAC (*Union douanière et économique de l'Afrique*) and to ask France for military assistance.[124] On 28 October

1981, Goukouny said that the "man in the street" in Chad is hostile to the Libyans.[125] Two days later, Goukouny formally asked the Libyans to withdraw their troops by the end of the year.[126]

In the South Vice-President Kamougué broke with the Libyans, who had supported him during 1979-1980, and called on the Sara to resist the Libyan presence in Chad. Like Tombalbaye, Malloum, Habré, Siddiq, Goukouny and Mahamt Abba before him — Kamougué too discovered that it was difficult to survive on the back of the Libyan tiger. In 1981 the South, which in the 1960s and 1970s had been relatively unified compared with the fragmented North, began to break apart. Again — as in the North since 1975 — the attitude towards Libya became a major dividing line between the various Southern factions. Regional, ethnic, tribal and personal conflicts which were contained as long as the South faced the North in the civil war, came to the fore and contributed their share to the growing disunity within the South. One group in the South felt betrayed by their longtime French allies who did not prevent the Northern takeover and the Libyan invasion. They regarded Habré's faction, which had slaughtered thousands of Saras in 1979, as their worst enemy, while the Libyans were considered the lesser evil. Another group disagreed and regarded the Libyan menace as a mortal danger to the non-Muslim South. This group which was led by Doudou Kemto and his *Mouvement Patriotique National* (MPN) called for armed warfare against the Libyans. In between these groups there were Djogo's and Kamougué's factions. The split in the South was in no way indicative of any support for unification.[127]

In the North, Habré's FAN continued throughout 1981 to fight the Libyan troops. As in the past, Habré skillfully played the racial card, accusing the Libyans of committing genocide against the blacks.[128] In addition to FAN, other groupings — such as Siddiq's FROLINAT originel, Sanūsi's FROLINAT fondmental and Moussa Medela's FAO — joined the forces resisting the Libyans. Medela, who was GUNT Minister of Health fled to Sudan in May 1981, and reported that an all out war between GUNT and the Libyans had become inevitable.[129] Medela's FAO accused the Libyans of "harassing civilians and despoiling the country of its riches".[130] On 2 September 1981 *Le Monde* reported the conclusion of an anti-Libyan alliance between the Southern MPN and three Northern groupings (FROLINAT originel, FROLINAT fondamental and the MPLT). Thus Libya's policy in Chad triggered a previously inconceivable development — the uniting of Northerners and Southerners on a common Chadian nationalist platform. Rumours circulated in the summer of 1981 about Libyan threats to liquidate Goukouny[131] and about secret contacts between Habré and Goukouny with the aim to re-establish the anti-Libyan coalition of 1979 (GUNT I).[132] All reports recorded Libyan unpopularity even in the Chadian North. A factor which very much weakened the anti-Libyan forces were the personal clashes and splits within the rebel forces. Nevertheless, FAN, which was supported by Egyptian supplies and military advisers, remained throughout 1981 a formidable force.[133]

In November 1981 the Libyan forces began to withdraw from Chad. The Libyan leaders, who always argued that they had been invited to Chad by Goukouny's legitimate government, had now to heed Goukouny's public demands for their withdrawal. Qadhdhā-fī's surprising retreat owes also much to the pressures of the OAU which decided to apply stick and carrot tactics in order to get the Libyan troops out of Chad. Qadhdhāfī was elected OAU Chairman for 1982 and Tripoli was chosen for the next OAU summit, but these "carrots" were accompanied by "sticks" — threats to boycott Tripoli if the Libyans did not withdraw from Chad. The rise to power of Mitterand in France also changed the situation. In contrast to Giscard d'Estaing's policies, the socialist government was more ready to apply economic sanctions against Qadhdhāfī's Libya. When the Libyans started to withdraw from Ndjamena and the eastern Sahel, Asīl protested in vain that the situation was not "ripe" for a Libyan withdrawal. Without Libyan protection his CDR forces were vulnerable to attacks by FAN and on 19 November 1981, Habré indeed regained Abéché, Ouaddai's old capital and the major town in the eastern Sahel.

X

LIBYA'S FOREIGN POLICY IN AFRICA:
The Case of Chad

There are five political-ideological dimensions to Qadhdhāfī's policies in Africa: Libyan state interests, pan-Arabism, pan-Islamism, anti-Westernism and identification with the Sahara and the Sahel.[134] Narrow economic and strategic considerations define the Libyan state interests. Qadhdhāfī's pan-Arabism, pan-Islamism and anti-Westernism echo the prevailing political ideologies of Qadhdhāfī's formative years in the 1950s and the 1960s, when the political climate of the region was strongly influenced by Nasser's calls to unify the Arab world, to mobilize the political power of Islam and to fight Western colonialism and imperialism. Nasser's *Philosophy of Revolution* and the pan-Arab agitation of Radio Cairo in the 1950s made a strong impact on the young Qadhdhāfī. The major difference between Nasser's and Qadhdhāfī's concepts of Arab nationalism and Arab unity lies in Qadhdhāfī's orientation towards the Sahara and the Sahel. Qadhdhāfī himself comes from a Beduin tribe in the Libyan Sahara. He is a man of the Sahara and has deep emotional ties to the Saharan population. Qadhdhāfī's own contribution to pan-Arabism is the adoption of the Touaregs, Berbers, Toubous and other Saharan ethnic groups into the Arab nation.[135] His origins in the arabised Berber Qadhdhāfā tribe may explain his expansive and flexible concept of the Arab nation.[136] Thus Qadhdhāfī's pan-Arabism differs from that of Nasser, who regarded the *Mashriq* and the *Maghrib* as components of the Arab world, but not the Sahara and Sahel.

Common to all dimensions of Libyan foreign policy is the aspiration to enlarge Libyan, Arab and Muslim power. An analysis of Libya's foreign policy in Africa reveals that circumstances determine which dimensions become dominant and which become secondary or even dormant at a specific moment.

a. Libyan State Interests

In authoritarian régimes the government tends to identify its own interests, particularly that of survival, with those of the state. Accordingly, the survival of Qadhdhāfī's régime was an important factor in shaping Libya's foreign policy. Qadhdhāfī, therefore, attempted to prevent the encircling of Libya by forces hostile to him and to remove foreign bases, which he deemed dangerous to his regime's security, from the neighbouring countries.

Libya's readiness to come to terms with France in Chad in 1971-1972 as a *quid pro quo* for the 110 Mirages is an example demonstrating that Libyan state interests have temporarily over-ridden ideological commitments.

The Aouzou Strip affair is another case in point. The Libyan occupation and annexation of the Strip had not a predominantly pan-Arab, pan-Islamic or anti-colonial rationale. It had a Libyan rationale. The Strip contains rich uranium deposits vital for Libya's nuclear projects and for the development of the Pakistani "Islamic bomb", a project in which Libya is involved[137].

The bitter rivalry between Qadhdhāfī's Libya and Sadat's Egypt added another strategic factor to Libya's policies in Chad. Chad is the soft underbelly of Libya as much as Sudan is the soft underbelly of Egypt. The Libyan presence in Chad had thus a double function — one offensive and one defensive. Chad is an ideal stepping stone for infiltrating and destabilizing Sudan and Egypt, and at the same time a Libyan presence in Chad prevents it from becoming a base of operations for the enemies of Qadhdhāfī's régime.

Egypt's support for Malloum (1975-1978), the Dual Government (1978-1979), GUNT I (1979) and, lately, for Habré's FAN has shown a consistent Egyptian policy to support Qadhdhāfī's enemies in Chad. In this context it is possible to appreciate Libya's chief of Staff, Brig. Gen. Abu Bakr Yūnis Jābir, who defended the Chadian invasion as a precautionary move to prevent the "encircling of the Great 1 September Revolution".[138] Qadhdhāfī's support for Kamougué's Southern Christians in 1979-1980 further demonstrated that, at certain moments, security interests and strategic balance of power calculations overrode religious solidarity, even in the external relations of Islamic fundamentalist Libya.

Libya has pursued also its narrow economic interest in Africa and elsewhere. Even in periods of intense hostility toward "French colonialism" and "American imperialism" it continued to sell its oil to those countries. Libya has invested large sums of money to buy a stake in the diamond and shipping industries, the iron ore fields, and in banking throughout West Africa. Certainly, the economic weapon was frequently employed for political ends, but economic interests *per se* were also important. Qadhdhāfī has faced, in recent years, bitter disputes with Tunisia and Malta over oil exploration rights in the Mediterranean. It is probable too that the economic variable played a role in the Chad situation. The Aouzou Strip is rich not only in uranium (which is not only a strategic but also an economic asset), but also in other minerals like copper, tungsten, zinq and wolfram. In Kanem, rich oil reserves were discovered and a host of oil companies (Shell, Exxon, Chevron and Conoco) were vigorously exploring the promising oilfields. It is a well-known secret that Libya's oil reserves will be exhausted by the end of the century, and hence the takeover of the Chadian oil reserves may thus be of prime economic importance to Libya. Throughout the 1970s Libyan pressures to found joint Libyan–Chadian companies for the exploration of the mines in the B.E.T. region indicate that economic calculations also motivated Libyan actions.

b. Pan-Arabism

Pan-Arabism is fundamental to Qadhdhāfī's *Weltanschaung*. The fragility of Libya's national identity, the traditional division of Libya into Tripolitania, Cyrenaica and the Fezzan and the fact that the Libyan political entity is a recent historical phenomenon make Arabism and Islam the natural focal points for any Libyan natio-alism. Qadhdhāfī always refers to the Libyan *Arab* Republic, the great *Arab* nation, the *Arab* Homeland and *Arab* Destiny. The centrality of the Palestine issue in Libyan foreign policy also has its roots in Qadhdhāfī's strong commitment to pan-Arabism. As was the case with Nasser, Qadhdhāfī's foreign policy is marked by a series of futile efforts to unify the Arab world. During his first three years in power (1969-1972) Qadhdhāfī's pan-Arab zeal was directed to the Arab East (*Mashriq*). In February 1970, a Federal Union between Libya, Egypt and the Sudan was established. In April 1971, the Confederation of Arab Republics consisting of

Libya, Egypt and Syria, was founded. In August 1972, Qadhdhāfī and Sādāt called for a merger between Egypt and Libya. All those efforts ended in failure. A turning point with regard to "unification" with Egypt was the fiasco of the people's march into Egypt in July 1973, a march through which Qadhdhāfī and the Libyan "masses" sought to force a merger against Egypt's inclination and better judgement. The final break with Egypt came in the aftermath of the October 1973 war, when Egypt reached a series of agreements with Israel.

Libya, disillusioned with the *Mashriq* turned to the Arab West (*Maghrib*). In January 1974, what proved to be a shortlived union with Tunisia was announced. Offers to Algeria followed later. But these efforts were also abortive. Faced with failures in the *Mashriq* and *Maghrib*, Qadhdhāfī then turned southwards to the Arab and Arabised Sahara to realize his pan-Arab dreams. The "unification" with Chad, and the growing Libyan involvement in Mauritania and the Western Sahara were a direct result of Libya's failures to merge with its neighbours to the east (Egypt and Sudan) and to the west (Tunisia and Algeria). Nevertheless, Libya did not relinquish Nasser's vision of an Arab empire from the Atlantic Ocean to the Arab (Persian) Gulf. An indication of this was the "union" with Syria which was announced in September 1980. Qadhdhāfī only changed the tactics, namely to accumulate power by creating a Libyan-led Saharan–Arab bloc which might then use its power resources to attract other states in the *Mashriq* and *Maghrib* to a greater pan-Arab state. Qadhdhāfī's African policies reflect not only Libyan state interests but also the vision of pan-Arabism. Pan-Arab solidarity further explains Qadhdhāfī's zeal in trying to remove the Israeli presence from the whole of Africa. In Chad, too, Qadhdhāfī regarded the eradication of the Israeli presence and influence as one of his major aims. In November 1972 Qadhdhāfī's Arab nationalist interest to have the Israelis expelled from Chad, even led to a tactical arrangement with the "neo-colonial" Tombalbaye and at least a temporary reduction of support for FROLINAT. With regard to Chad, Libya emphasized its Arab character, and explained the Libyan involvement as an Arab brotherly act towards the Arab people of Chad.[139] In Qadhdhāfī's eyes the arabised Saharan and Sahelian parts of Chad are part and parcel of the "Great Arab Homeland". Libya's staunchest allies in Chad are Asīl and his followers — all of them ethnic Arabs from the Sahel. Thus, to a certain extent, the attempted "unification" of January 1981 had its roots not only in Libyan state interests but also in Qadhdhāfī's concept of pan-Arabism.

c. Pan-Islam

Qadhdhāfī's pan-Islamic convictions complement his Arab nationalism. While Nasser's attitude towards Islam was that of a secular nationalist who used religion for his nationalist purposes, Qadhdhāfī's Islam is more authentic and forceful. Nasser never called on Christian Arabs to convert to Islam nor did he ever maintain that only a Muslim Arab is a true Arab. Qadhdhāfī did both. For him, no distinction exists between Arabism and Islam. His fundamental, Islamic orthodox policies inside Libya are reflected in his foreign policy. Qadhdhāfī has supported rebellious Muslim minorities in Thailand and the Philippines. Qadhdhāfī also wholeheartedly supported the Islamic Revolution in Iran. Throughout the world — and particularly in Africa — Libya has financed the construction of mosques and the establishment of Islamic Schools and Study Centres. In the African continent, Qadhdhāfī is interested first and foremost in neighbouring Arab states (Egypt, Sudan, Algeria, Tunisia), in more distant Arab countries (Morocco, Mauritania, Western Sahara) and in the wholly or partially Arabised Sahel belt (Chad, Niger, Mali). Another group of states where Qadhdhāfī's Libya is meddling in internal policies are the Muslim states in West-Africa and the Horn of Africa. Libya is also involved with Muslim minorities in predominantly non-Muslim states. His pan-Islamic fervour does not allow Qadhdhāfī to limit his ambition and activity to Arab and arabised Africa. South of the Muslim line in Africa, there is a sharp decline in the intensity of the Libyan involvement.

A few examples will suffice to demonstrate his activities in Muslim Black Africa: In Muslim Gambia, pro-Libyan *coup d'états* were foiled in October 1980 and August 1981. In Senegal, Libya has actively supported the Muslim movement of Ahmat Khalifa Niasse, the *Marabout* (called *"Ayatollah"*) of Kaolack. Niasse, who lives in Libya, has recruited Senegalese Muslims who are being trained in Libyan bases to fight for the creation of an Islamic Republic in Senegal.[140] In Uganda, Qadhdhāfī sent thousands of

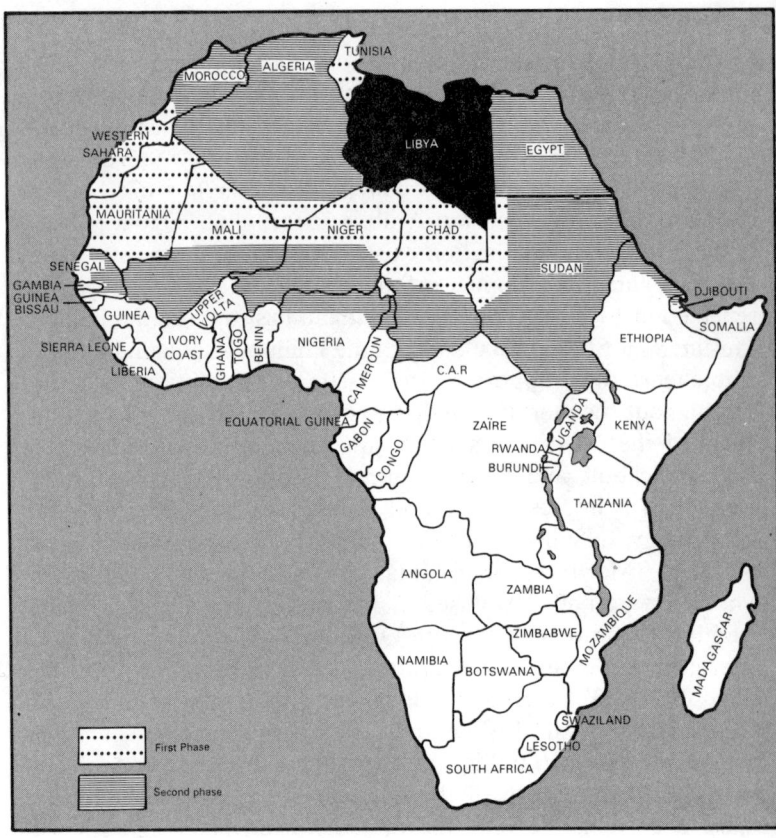

Map No. 3: The Planned Libyan Sphere of Influence

his troops to save his fellow Muslim Idi Amin. In Nigeria, reports said that Libyan agents had recruited mercenaries in the Muslim north, that Libyan money flowed to the coffers of Muslim associations and parties and that Libyan agitators were involved in riots in Kano in December 1980.[141] In Upper Volta the deposed President Lamizana claimed, before his downfall, that the Libyans were subverting his government.[142]

Libya also created an Islamic army of Arabic-speaking Muslims recruited mainly from African countries. The army consists of recruits from Egypt, Sudan, Tunisia, Morocco, Chad, Niger, Mali, Senegal, Nigeria, and the Ivory Coast, and is being trained by Soviets, Cubans and Palestinians. The Islamic army has already been employed in the defence of Amin in Uganda (April 1979), in the attack on the Tunisian town of Gafsa (January 1980) and in the invasion of Chad.[143]

In Chad, the Islamic factor certainly played an important role in shaping Libyan policy. Qadhdhāfī identified himself with the struggle of the Muslim North, although tactics and Libyan *raison d'état* also led to temporary betrayals. In the 1970s, Libya tried to strike a bargain with France on the partition of Chad into spheres of influence. Qadhdhāfī was willing to incorporate only the Muslim North into Libya's sphere while "conceding" the black Christians and the Pagans in the South to the French.

In 1978-1981 Libya became involved in Southern politics because the South plays a role in Chadian alignments and realignments. Nevertheless, Libyan troops did not penetrate into the South and, in 1979, Qadhdhāfī even supported the potentially separatist Kamougué with arms and ammunition. There can hardly be any doubt that Qadhdhāfī's prime interest in Chad is with his fellow Muslims in the North.[144]

d. Anti-Westernism

Qadhdhāfī's foreign policy is fiercely opposed to "colonialism", "neo-colonialism", the "imperialist" Western Great Powers and their conservative ("moderate" in western parlance) allies in the Arab world and Black Africa. Libya's recent history was marked by Italian colonial rule from 1911 to 1942, a period of settler colonialism and fascist brutality. Later on Libya experienced also the humiliating British and French rule in the North and in the southern Fezzan respectively. British and American military base — detested symbols of Western imperialism — were established in Libya after the Second World War and only removed in 1969 after Qadhdhāfī's revolution.

Qadhdhāfī's radical government aspired to emulate Nasser' "Arab Socialism" and became part of the radical *camp* in the Arab world. Hence Libya became a sworn enemy of the traditionalist pro-Western monarchies. in the region. It was involved in attempted *coup d'états* against King Hassan in Morocco, supported the PLO in its showdown with King Hussein's Jordan, assisted the POLISARIO in its fight in the Western Sahara, allied itself with radical South Yemen against conservative Oman, opposed Sādāt' pro-Western policies and assisted the leftist *Popular Front* and *Popular Democratic Front* against the Saudi-financed PLO establishment.

In Black Africa too, Libya belongs to the radical camp which has close relations with the Soviet bloc and raises the anti-Western flag everywhere (It is interesting to note that even King Idris' Libya belonged to the radical *Casablanca Group* and not to the moderate *Monrovia Bloc*). Libya's closest supporters in Africa are radical states such as Guinea, Benin and Congo. Libya supported the pro-Soviet Somalis and Erithreans against pro-Western Ethiopia in the Haile Selassie era, but switched sides after the establishment of a pro-Soviet regime in Addis Ababa and Somalia's turning to the West. Libya has trained African guerrillas from Mozambique Angola, Zimbabwe and Namibia. Recently, Libya offered to send troops to aid SWAPO to liberate Namibia. Qadhdhāfī has also supported armed revolutionaries in pro-Western, African states. Examples are the *Somali Salvation Front*, the *Lesotho Liberation Army* and Zaire's *Peoples' Revolutionary Party*.

Qadhdhāfī has always regarded the French presence in West and Central Africa as an obstacle to the achievement of his aims in the Sahara and the Sahel. The African "puppet governments" of France, the French control of the African economies, the French military bases and the French troops in the area have always been regarded by Libyan rulers as manifestation of colonialist "aggression, plunder and exploitation"[145] which have to be eliminated

In the 1960s and 1970s Chad represented such a neo-colonial entity in which the French controlled the government, the economy, the army and the security services. French troops were stationed in Chad until May 1980. Libyan support for FROLINAT in the Tombalbaye and Malloum eras also reflected the Libyan desire — shared in the 1970s by Qadhdhāfī's Soviet supporters — to unseat the pro-French "neo-colonial" establishment in Chad and to bring to power anti-Western forces. Both the Libyans and the Soviets wished to see the fall of the pro-Western governments in West and Central Africa.

Libyan caution regarding its Chadian policies in the 1970s stemmed from the basic conflict between its anti-imperialism and its other Libyan and Arab interests. The role of France as Libya's arms supplier, French oil interests there and the pro-Arab policies of Gaullist France, go far to explain Libya's hesitant moves in the 1970s as well as its tactical retreats and temporary compromises with the "French puppets" in Ndjamena. The 1972 Qadhdhāfī–Tombalbaye transaction and the 1978 Benghazi Accords are representative of Qadhdhāfī's policies which are cautious and calculated.

Nevertheless, it remained Libya's aim to eliminate the French presence in Chad, but to do it in such a way so as to avoid both a military confrontation and a break in the lucrative trade with France. In that respect Qadhdhāfī's policy in 1980-1981 was entirely successful. When Libyan tanks rolled into Ndjamena and "unification" was proclaimed, Libyan pilots were training in France, French arms continued to pour into Libya, 1,800 French experts were working in Libya and the French governmental *Elf-Aquitaine* was negotiating oil concessions in Tripoli.[146]

In spite of angry French declaratrions and dramatic troop movements, Qadhdhāfī succeeded in having his cake and eating it, occupying Chad without precipitating a rupture with France.

e. Identification with the Sahara and the Sahel

Libya's special relationship with the Sahara and the Sahel has geographical and historical origins. Pre-colonial trade routes from the Sahel led to Benghazi and Tripoli, and the Libyan Fezzan had always had ethnic, religious and political connections with present-day Niger, Mali and Chad. Furthermore, Qadhdhāfī perceived an internal power vacuum in the Sahara, which was a result of the sparse population and small armies of the Saharan and Sahelian states. Qadhdhāfī regarded the Sahara–Sahel belt as part of the

Arab world. In the late 1970s, after the failure of his unification plans in the *Mashriq* and *Maghrib*, he came to perceive the Sahara and the Sahel as the area where his ambitions for unification might meet the least resistance. Qadhdhāfī also denies the legitimacy of the colonial boundaries,[147] because in the Sahel states they group together Arab or arabised regions with black African areas. This is the case in Mauritania, Niger, Mali, Chad and the Sudan where there is an Arab or arabised North and an African, non-Arab South (which in the case of Chad and Sudan is also non-Muslim). For African leaders who support the sanctity of the colonial borders, Qadhdhāfī's stand on the question of boundaries is heretical. Qadhdhāfī's readiness to support separatist or irredentist tendencies among the Touaregs in northern Niger and Mali, which are "minorities" according to his "Green Book", who "need to return to their own nations and homelands,[148] explain the Sahel states' fear of the Libyan *qaid* (leader).

Qadhdhāfī has declared all Touaregs to be Libyans[149] and has called on the Touaregs of both countries to rise against their oppressors — the black African governments of Moussa Traoré and Seyni Kountché.[150] Libya is constantly meddling in Mauritanian affairs by nurturing a pro-Libyan faction in the ruling moorish élite. The intensive involvement in the internal politics of the Western Sahara POLISARIO stems from Libya's ambition to bring the exile government of the Saharan Arab Democratic Republic within its pan-Arab schemes.

Libya's polcies in Chad are more readily understood knowing that in Qadhdhāfī's eyes not only the ethnic Arabs, but also the Toubous, Massalit, Kanembous and other Northerners form part of the Arab nation. Turaykī's remark about the "historic, geographic and spiritual relations between the Arab Libyan and Chadian peoples"[151] should not be discarded as mere propaganda. It reflects genuine sentiments. The strategic location of Chad as a key factor for any Saharan "unification" under Libyan hegemony, make the events of January 1981 even more explicable.

APPENDIX

LIBYA–CHAD COMMUNIQUÉ ON UNIFICATION

LD061852 Tripoli Domestic Service in Arabic 1600 GMT 6 Jan 81.

("Text" of joint communiqué on visit to Libya of Goukouni Oueddei, president of Chad, issued in Tripoli on 6 January)[152]

(Text) At the invitation of the brother Col. Mu'ammar al-Qadhdhāfī, leader of the great Fatah revolution, the head of the Provisional National Unity Government of Chad and head of state, President Goukouni Oueddei, paid an official visit to the Socialist People's Libyan Arab Jamahiriyah between 26-30 Safar 1390 since the death of the prophet, corresponding to 2-6 January 1981, heading an important government delegation.

The guest and accompanying delegation were accorded a great, fraternal welcome which expressed the depth of fraternal ties between the two fraternal peoples.

President Goukouni Oueddei took part in the opening session of the third session of the General People's Congress. He made an important speech dealing with the Socialist People's Libyan Arab Jamahiriyah's pioneering role in supporting legality in Chad and exposing the role of reaction and some agent regimes in fanning the flames of sedition among the ranks of the people of Chad. On the occasion, he denounced the dubious role of As-Sadat's regime and that of Numayri against the will of the Chadian people, when they sided with the rebel Habré and supported him militarily and materially, stressing that stand was an application of the plans of colonialism. This being the case, he stressed that harboring the rebel Habré in any place is regarded as an act of aggression against the Chadian people.

Proceeding from the historic, cultural, human, racial, geographical and spiritual relations between the two fraternal Arab Libyan and Chadian peoples, and out of their belief in the unity of the common fate of the two peoples and so as to emobdy the eternal principles of the great Fatah revolution and the Frolinat revolution, the two sides stress that relations between the two peoples have their roots in these historic, geographical and spiritual ties: both peoples fought colonialism in Libya and in Chad side by side; their bood was shed for the same cause. The two peoples have mixed together over a long period of history. Tens of thousands of Chadian people have lived in Libya and have become Libyans, tens of thousands of Libyans have lived in Chad and have become Chadians.

Within the framework of the strategic alliance between the Socialist People's Libyan Arab Jamahiriyah and Chad, important talks took place between the leadership of both countries.

During these talks, it was agreed:

1. To work for the realization of complete unity between the two countries — a jamahiri (masses) unity in which authority, arms and resources are in the hands of the people; its (foundation) is the people's congresses and committees.

2. To support the strategic and fateful alliance between the two countries, and to regard any aggression on either as an aggression on the other; each country is prepared to fight on the side of the other in case of an aggression on either of them.

3. The two sides decided to continue to support the struggle of the peoples struggling for their freedom, and to escalate the struggle against colonialism and Zionism and reaction in Africa and the Arab homeland, as everywhere else in the world.

4. The Socialist People's Libyan Arab Jamahiriyah stresses the continuation of its support for the fraternal Republic of Chad in order to ensure the freedom and independence of its people and to eliminate the remnants of agent reaction which co-operates with colonialism, inside and outside.

5. Proceedings from the joint defense treaty signed between the two countries on 2 Sha'ban 1389 since the death of the prophet, corresponding to 15 June 1980, and in accordance with the official request of the Government of Chad, the Socialist People's Libyan Arab Jamahiriyah will send a number of military men to assist in keeping security and maintaining peace, which have been realized by the ending of the civil war, and also to assist in the rebuilding of a Chadian National Army and Chadian security forces.

6. Both sides stress their complete condemnation of reactionary, imperialist and Zionist attempts, which are supported by colonial-

ism, in the region, and in particular the two agent regimes in Egypt and Sudan, which seek to do harm to the victories scored by the Chadian people and to rekindle the flames of war and sedition in Chad.

The activities which are being practiced by the Egyptian and Sudanese regimes and the Sudanese president's statement that war has now begun in Chad are regarded as an embarking on aggression against the Chadian people, and are preparatory agent measures for aggression on Chad. What the two regimes are doing violates the principles of the OAU Charter and the Lagos agreement. In this connection, the two sides warn the Sudanese regime against the serious consequences of any aggressive act against Chad from Sudanese territory. The Sudanese regime shall be held responsible for the consequences. The Chadian people will not remain indifferent to what can be regarded as a threat to its security and safety.

7. The Jamahiriyah stresses the continuation of and the increase in its economic support for sister Chad in order to rebuild Chad and realize prosperity and progress for the fraternal Chadian people.

8. The two sides express full satisfaction with co-operation between the Socialist People's Libyan Arab Jamahiriyah and Chad, a matter which effectively contributed to the realisation of peace and security in the sister Republic of Chad.

9. The two sides express pleasure at the positive results which were achieved by the recent Lagos conference on the Chadian issue stressing their commitment to the resolutions which were adopted by the conference and which stress without a shadow of doubt the ability of the Africans to resolve their problems by themselves without any foreign and colonialist intervention.

In this regard, the two sides express thanks and appreciation for the valuable efforts which were exerted by the sister Nigerian Federal Republic and its President Alhaji Shehu Shagari to realize peace in Chad, and all of their appreciation of the current OAU chairman and Sierra Leone President, Siaka Stevens.

10. The Chadian side highly appreciates the aid which the Jamahiriyah has given the Chad people, thanks to which the

Chadian people were able to put an end to the rebels and to realize peace and security in Chad.

11. The two sides have decided to open the borders between the Socialist People's Libyan Arab Jamahiriyah and the Chadian republic so as to enable Libyan and Chadian citizens to move with full freedom and without any restrictions in order to realize cohesion and interaction between the two fraternal people.

12. The two sides stress the importance of supporting the legitimate government in Chad, it being the sole legitimate authority in Chad. They call on the African states and the international community to support this government, so as to enable it to rebuild Chad, and also to give it aid and to completely refrain from dealing with any side or sides outside this government.

13. The two sides stress their commitment to work to preserve security and stability in the region, and also to respect the political choices of the countries of the region and the will of their governments, and also their adherence to the principles of non-interference in the internal affairs of other countries.

The Chadian Government expresses the desire to promote its relations with all states, and in particular those neighboring Chad, provided that these states respect the sovereignty of Chad and refrain from interfering in its internal affairs.

LIST OF ABBREVIATIONS

B.E.T.	Borkou — Ennedi — Tibesti
PPT	Parti Progressiste Tchadien
UDT	Union Démocratique Tchadienne
AST	Action Sociale Tchadienne
PSIC	Parti Socialiste Indépendant du Chad
RDA	Rassemblement Démocratique Africain
MSA	Mouvement Socialiste Africain
UST	Union Socialiste Tchadienne
PNA	Parti National Africain
UPT	Union pour le Progrès du Tchad
FROLINAT	Front pour la Libération Nationale du Tchad
UNT	Union Nationale Tchadienne
FLT	Front Libération Tchadienne
FAN	Forces Armées du Nord
CSM	Conseil Supérieur Militaire
CDS	Comité de Défense et de Sécurité
FAT	Forces Armées Tchadiennes
FAP	Forces Armées Populaires
CDR	Conseil Démocratique de la Révolution
MPLT	Mouvement pour la Libération du Tchad
GUNT	Gouvernement d'Union Nationale de Transition
FLP	Forces de Libération Populaire
FAC (P)	Front d'Action Commune (Provisoire)
FAO	Forces Armées de l'Occident
ANI	Armée Nationale Integrée
MPN	Mouvement Patriotique National
UDEAC	Union Douanière et Economique de l'Afrique Central
SWAPO	South West African People's Organisation

NOTES

1.   As in the Middle East and North Africa Islam in Northern Chad is a central factor in any collective political identity, while in West and East Africa (e.g. in Western Nigeria, Upper Volta, Northern Ghana, Tanzania) the political importance of Islam is marginal. Chadian Islam is regarded as Arabised because its religious leadership has been trained in Egypt, Sudan and Libya, because the Arabic language is widely spoken among the Muslims and because it is connected with the Arab civilization of North Africa. On Islam in Africa see V. Monteil *Islam noir* (Paris, 1964), I.M. Lewis (ed.) *Islam in Tropical Africa* (London, Oxford University Press 1966), S. Trimingham *Islam in West Africa* (London, Oxford University Press 1959) and *Islam in East Africa* (London, Oxford University Press 1964).

2.   J. Le Cornec, *Histoire Politique du Tchad de 1900 à 1962* (Paris, Pichon et Durand — Anzias 1963), pp. 4-5.

3.   N. Levtzion, *Islam as a Political Factor in Chad* (Jerusalem, Hebrew University, Department of African Studies, n.d.), pp. 3-6.

4.   R. Buijtenhuis, "La dialectique Nord-Sud dans l'histoire tchadienne", *African Perspectives* No. 2 (1977), p. 45.

5.   M.F.v. Oppenheim, *Rabeh und das Tschadseegebiet* (Berlin, Reimer 1902), pp. 26-27.

6.   H.D. Nelson and others, *Area Handbook for Chad* (Washington, US Government 1972), p. 75.

7.   V. Oppenheim, *op. cit.*, p. 31.

8.   V. Thompson and R. Adloff, *The Emerging States of French Equatorial Africa* (Stanford, Stanford University Press 1960), pp. 431-436.

9.   R. Buijtenhuis, *Le Frolinat et les révoltes populaires du Tchad* (The Hague, Mouton 1978), pp. 21-35.

10. T.A. Marks, "Lessons France Learnt in Chad" *Africa Institute Bulletin*, V. 16 No. 3 (1978), p. 124.

11. Until 1935 France followed in the North an "anti-Sultan" policy aimed to dismantle the traditional kingdoms and to weaken the traditional political élite. From 1935 the French followed a "grand turbans" policy — a system of indirect rule with the help of the traditional chiefs and Sultans. This also brought about a change in the character and quality of the French colonial administrators in the North. See R. Buijtenhuis, "La dialectique Nord-Sud dans l'histoire tchadienne", *op.cit.*, p. 50.

12. S. Decalo, "Regionalism, Political Decay and Civil Strife in Chad", *Journal of Modern African Studies*, v. 18 No. 1 (1980), pp. 40-41.

13. *Africa Contemporary Record* 1969/1970, p. B394.
14. G. Gera, *The Qaddafi Regime in Libya: Ideological and Social Origins and Practice*, Thesis, Tel Aviv University 1978 (Hebrew), p. 411.
15. Y. Wright, *Libya* (London, E. Benn 1969), pp. 112-113.
16. J. Ferrandi, *Le Centre African Francais* (Paris, Lavenzelle 1930), pp. 31, 167, 215.
17. Y. Berri et S. Kebzabo, "Que Fait Khaddafi au Tchad?" *Jeune Afrique* 768 (26/9/1975), p. 19.
18. *Africa Contemporary Record* 1970/1971, p. B282.
19. *Africa Research Bulletin* v. 8 No. 9 (15/10/1971), p. 2217.
20. *West Africa* 24/9/1971.
21. *West Africa* 22/10/1971.
22. *Africa Research Bulletin* V. 8 no. 8 (15/9/1971), p. 2200.
23. *West Africa* 10/9/1971, 22/10/1971.
24. *West Africa* 24/9/1971.
25. *Africa Research Bulletin* V. 8 No. 9 (15/10/1971), p. 2217.
26. *West Africa* 1/10/1971.
27. *Africa Research Bulletin* V. 9 No. 2 (15/3/1971), p. 2369.
28. S. Decalo *op.cit.*, p. 42.
29. *Africa Contemporary Record*, 1972/1973, pp. B519-527.
30. *Africa Contemporary Record*, 1974/1975, p. B568.
31. *Africa Research Bulletin*, V. 12 No. 4 (15/5/1977), pp. 3593-3596.
32. *West Africa,,* 20/9/1976.
33. *Africa Research Bulletin*, V. 13 No. 10 (15/10/1976), p. 4182.
34. *Marchés Tropicaux et Méditerranéens*, V. 31 No. 1559 (26/9/1975), pp. 2377-2678.
35. *Afrique Contemporaine*, No. 39 (Sept.-Oct. 1977), pp. 17-19.
36. *Jeune Afrique*, No. 768 (26/9/1975).
37. *Africa*, No. 88 (December 1978).
38. Tombalbaye's "Cultural Revolution" was an imitation of Mobutu's policies in Zaire. Tombalbaye wanted to demonstrate his commitment to African nationalism by a return to indigenous, pre-colonial non-Christian traditions, rites and names. During the "Cultural Revolution" Fort Lamy became Ndjamena and Francois Tombalbaye became Ngarta Tombalbaye. All this was intended to refute Tombalbaye's image as a "neo-colonial puppet".
39. *Africa Institute Bulletin*, V. 13 (1975), 149-151.
40. *West Africa*, 12/7/1976.
41. *Africa Research Bulletin*, V. 12 No. 4 (15/5/1975), pp. 3593-3597.
42. *Africa Research Bulletin*, V. 14 No. 7 (15/8/1977), pp. 4492-3 and V. 15 No. 7 (15/8/1978), p. 4913.
43. *Africa Research Bulletin*, V. 15 No. 7 (15/8/1978), pp. 4487-4488.

44.   *Africa Research Bulletin*, V. 13 No. 4 (15/5/1976), p. 3996.
45.   R. Buijtenhuis, *Le Frolinat et les révoltes populaires du Tchad 1965-1978*, p. 308.
46.   *Africa Research Bulletin*, V. 14 No. 4 (15/5/1977), pp. 4392-3.
47.   *Africa Contemporary Record*, 1977/1978, p. B 546.
48.   *West Africa*, 27/7/1977.
49.   *Africa*, No. 80 (April 1980).
50.   L. Bontemps, "Nord et Sud dans l'évolution politique du Tchad" *Afrique Contemporaine*" No. 99 (Sept.-Oct. 1978), pp. 1-7.
51.   *Africa Research Bulletin*, V. 15 No. 6 (15/7/1978), p. 4884.
52.   *Afrique Contemporaine*, No. 98 (July–August 1978).
53.   *Jeune Afrique*, 24/12/1980.
54.   R. Buijtenhuis, *Le Frolinat et les révolts populaires du Tchad 1965-1978*, p. 279.
55.   *Conseil de Commandement des Forces Armées du Nord Document* (no publisher, 1977), pp. 4-5.
56.   Y. Berri et S. Kebzabo, *op.cit*, p. 21.
57.   *African Contemporary Record*, 1977/1978, p. B541.
58.   *Africa Report*, V. 24 No. 1 (January-February 1979).
59.   Radio Tripoli 25/1/1979 — *Daily Report* (DR), 26/1/1979.
60.   *Africa Research Bulletin*, V. 15 No. 9 (15/10/1978), pp. 4492-3.
61.   *Le Monde*, 24/4/1979.
62.   *Africa Research Bulletin*, V. 16 No. 2 (15/3/1979), pp. 5163, 5165.
63.   *Africa Report*, V. 23 No. 5 (September-October 1978).
64.   Radio Tripoli 1/5/1975, 2/5/1979, 18/5/1979, 29/5/1979 — *DR* 2/5/1979, 4/5/1979, 23/5/1979, 31/5/1979.
65.   Radio Tripoli 2/5/1979, 18/5/1979 — *DR* 4/5/1979, 23/5/1979.
66.   *Jeune Afrique*, 16/5/1979.
67.   *Afrique Contemporaine*, No. 103 (May-June 1979), p. 14.
68.   *Afrique Contemporaine*, No. 105 (September-October 1979).
69.   *Le Monde* 25/4/1979.
70.   *Africa* No. 96 (August 1979).
71.   *Arab Report* 9/5/1979; *New York Times* 21/4/1979.
72.   *Africa* No. 94 (June 1979), 95 (July 1979) and 96 (August 1979).
73.   *Afrique Contemporaine* No. 105 (September-October 1979), pp. 26-28. Organizations 6-11 formed on June 20, 1979, the *Front d'Action Commune Provisoire* (FACP). Later in the year *FROLINAT–originel* and *FROLINAT–fondamental* seceded from the FACP (also called the "Tripoli Group").
74.   *West Africa* 31/3/1980.
75.   *Africa Report*, V. 25 No. 5 (September-October 1980).
76.   *Afrique Contemporaine* No. 109 (May-June 1980).
77.   *West Africa* 21/4/1980.

78. Radio Paris 7/4/1980 — *DR* 8/4/1980.
79. Radio Paris 5/7/1980 — *DR* 8/7/1980.
80. *Africa* No. 10 (July 1980).
81. *West Africa* 13/10/1980, 22/12/1980.
82. Radio Tripoli 5/4/1980 — *DR* 7/4/1980.
83. *Jeune Afrique* 19/11/1980.
84. *Jeune Afrique* 21/1/1981.
85. Radio Tripoli 6/4/1980 — *DR* 7/4/1980.
86. Radio Tripoli 25/51980 — *DR* 27/5/1980.
87. Radio Paris 15/6/1980 — *DR* 16/6/1980; *The Times* 16/6/1981.
88. *Africa* No. 115 (March 1981).
89. *Jeune Afrique* 24/12/1980.
90. *Jeune Afrique* 21/1/1981 and *Africa Research Bulletin* 15/2/1981, pp. 5930, 5934.
91. *Jamahiriya Review* (December 1980), p. 9.
92. *Jamahiriya Review* (April 1981), p. 8.
93. *Ibid.*, pp. 9-10; Radio Tripoli 8/2/1981 — *DR* 9/2/1981.
94. *Africa Research Bulletin* 15/2/1981.
95. *Jeune Afrique* 21/1/1981.
96. *West Africa* 19/1/1981, 2/2/1981.
97. *Le Matin* 29/1/1981.
98. *Newsweek* 16/2/1981.
99. *Le Monde* 25-26/1/1981.
100. *Jeune Afrique* 21/1/1981.
101. *Jeune Afrique* 21/1/1981.
102. *Jeune Afrique* 21/1/1981.
103. *West Africa* 2/2/1981.
104. *West Africa* 2/3/1981.
105. *West Africa* 26/1/1981.
106. *Jeune Afrique* 11/3/1981.
107. *Africa Research Bulletin*, V. 16 No. 1 (15/2/1981), pp. 5933.
108. *Jamahiriya Review* (February 1981), p. 11.
109. Radio Paris 25/6/1981 — *DR* 25/6/1981.
110. *Jeune Afrique* 21/1/1981.
111. *Daily Report* 22/1/1981.
112. *Africa Research Bulletin*, V. 16 No. 1 (15/2/1981), p. 5933.
113. Radio Paris 13/1/1981 — *DR* 13/1/1981.
114. Radio Paris 23/3/1981 — *DR* 24/3/1981.
115. *Le Matin* 29/1/1981.
116. *Jamahiriya Review* (February 1981), p. 11.
117. *Al-Mujahid* 19/2/1981.
118. FACP later became FAC.
119. *Africa Research Bulletin* V. 18 No. 4 (15/5/1981), p. 6025.

120. *Le Monde* 20/10/1981.
121. Radio Paris 31/5/1981 — *DR* 2/6/1981.
122. Radio Paris 2/6/1981 — *DR* 3/6/1981.
123. *Le Monde* 15/9/1981.
124. *Le Monde* 27/10/1981, 29/10/1981.
125. *Le Monde* 27/10/1981.
126. *Le Monde* 31/10/1981.
127. *West Africa* 25/5/1981, 1/6/1981.
128. Radio Paris 7/4/1981 — *DR* 8/4/1981.
129. *Afrique Contemporaine* No. 115 (May-June 1981).
130. Radio Paris 20/6/1981 — *DR* 23/6/1981.
131. *Africa Research Bulletin* V. 18 No. 5 (15/6/1981), p. 6048.
132. *Internationales Afrika Forum* V. 17 No. 2 (summer 1981).
133. *Africa Research Bulletin* V. 18 No. 3 (15/4/1981), p. 5985. The Libyan Foreign Minister at-Turayki accused both Egypt and Israel of aiding Habré's FAN (See *'Al Nahār Al' 'Arabī Wa Al Duwalī* of February 16, 1981).
134. For a general discussion of Libya's foreign policy see also A. Nathan, "The Foreign policy of Libya", *Orbis* V. 24 No. 4 (1981), pp. 819-846 and J. Cooley "The Libyan Menace", *Foreign Policy*, No. 42 (1981), pp. 74-93.
135. *Jeune Afrique*, 11/2/1981.
136. *Area Handbook for Libya* (Washington 1973), pp. 97-99.
137. *Arabia and the Gulf*, 19/12/1977.
138. Radio Tripoli 17/6/1981 — *DR*, 18/6/1981.
139. *'Al-Nahar Al 'Arabi Wa Al Duwali*, 16/2/1981.
140. *West Africa* 21/7/1980, 10/11/1980.
141. *West Africa* 22/12/1980.
142. *The Economist* 29/11/1980.
143. *Le Monde* 13/2/1980; *Sunday Times* 7/2/1980.
144. That is also the view of Guy Georgy, for many years French ambassador in Libya (*Jeune Afrique* 11/2/1981).
145. Radio Tripoli 26/2/1978 — *DR* 3/3/1978.
146. *Jeune Afrique* 21/1/1981; 11/3/1981.
147. *Africa* No. 116 (March 1981).
148. Radio Tripoli 15/2/1981 — *DR* 17/2/1981.
149. *West Africa* 22/12/1981.
150. *Jeune Afrique* 4/2/1981.
151. *Washington Post* 16/8/1980.
152. *Daily Report* 7/1/1981.

Published in the Series

H. ERLICH: *The Universities in the Countries of the Arab World*, September 1981 (H).

Z. BAR LAVI: *The Hashimite Regime 1949-1967 and Its Status in the West Bank*, September 1981 (H).

U. DANN: *The Emirate of Transjordan, 1921-1946*, February 1982 (H).

Z. ELPELEG: *An "Independent Palestine" entangled in Inter-Arab Rivalries*, February 1982 (H).

H = Hebrew
E = English